FED
SAVVY

TOOLS AND TIPS TO MAXIMIZE YOUR FEDERAL BENEFITS

FED SAVVY

CAROL SCHMIDLIN

Advantage.

Published by Advantage, Charleston, South Carolina.
Member of Advantage Media Group.

ADVANTAGE is a registered trademark and the Advantage colophon is a trademark of Advantage Media Group, Inc.

Printed in the United States of America.

ISBN: 978-159932-297-1
LCCN: 2012930887

This publication is designed to provide accurate and authoritative information in regard to the subject matter covered. It is sold with the understanding that the publisher is not engaged in rendering legal, accounting, or other professional services. If legal advice or other expert assistance is required, the services of a competent professional person should be sought.

Advantage Media Group is proud to be a part of the Tree Neutral® program. Tree Neutral offsets the number of trees consumed in the production and printing of this book by taking proactive steps such as planting trees in direct proportion to the number of trees used to print books. To learn more about Tree Neutral, please visit www.treeneutral.com. To learn more about Advantage's commitment to being a responsible steward of the environment, please visit www.advantagefamily.com/green

Advantage Media Group is a leading publisher of business, motivation, and self-help authors. Do you have a manuscript or book idea that you would like to have considered for publication? Please visit www.amgbook.com or call 1.866.775.1696

It is my hope that this book will help you become aware of how you can maximize your Federal Employee Benefits, and other strategies to open the possibilities available to you and your family, enabling you to make your most important dreams come true with proper retirement planning.

Carol Schmidlin
Franklin Planning
123 Egg Harbor Rd.
Suite 303
Sewell, NJ 08080
(p)856-401-1101
www.franklinplanning.com

TABLE OF CONTENTS

SECTION 4: Entitlements, Social Security and Medicare

SECTION 5: Don't Just Survive – Thrive in Retirement

INTRODUCTION

"Half our life is spent trying to find

something to do with the time we have rushed

through life trying to save."

– Will Rogers

The Perfect Retirement Scenario: A generous pension, healthcare, life insurance, Thrift Savings Plan (TSP), along with many other benefits you can use towards your retirement. I am referring to the Civil Service Retirement System (CSRS) originated in 1920. The Federal Employees Retirement System (FERS) became effective in 1987, and almost all new federal civilian employees hired after 1983 are automatically covered by this new retirement system. Beginning January 1, 1984, new employees were required to pay into Social Security and pay into the Federal Employee Retirement System (FERS), which would pay a lower pension benefit, however, FERS would be able to collect Social Security. In addition they would get a match of up to 5% on their TSP contributions. And of course they could have healthcare and life insurance and all the other benefits of a federal career. The point is federal employees have really good benefits while working, and if they are willing to put in the time, will have some pretty nice retirement benefits.

At present, many federal employees are feeling threatened, and for good cause, because the Congressional Budget Office is dangling a knife over their benefits with several proposed cuts and packages that they believe will help reduce the United States' enormous deficit. Are your federal benefits at risk? Are we at the point of every man for himself?

While my guess is that some of these cuts may come to fruition, and you should fight for what is rightfully yours, you still have a pretty darn good retirement package. The problem is that federal benefits are complex and federal employees often have a hard time finding the information needed for them to make informed decisions about their financial future.

Many agencies have decentralized human resources. As a result, some federal employees no longer have a personal contact they can speak to. It's not that the information is not out there; they just don't know where to go, and even worse, how to interpret their findings.

The other problem is that the rules are always being updated and it's nearly impossible for the average worker to find the time to stay updated on how these changes may affect their work lives, their families, their income, retirement and quite frankly, their outlook on life.

The worst-case scenario is to take the path of least resistance and do nothing. This is typical for many of us when faced with financial decisions. The problem is by accepting the default position, especially with regard to retirement, you'll never know if you could have achieved greater financial security. Unlike so many other things in life, we don't get the chance to have a "do over" of our retirement.

My intent with this book is to identify the benefits that are specific from a financial planning aspect, and to share opportunities to help you maximize your federal benefits throughout your career and certainly into retirement. Many of you rely on your colleagues, family and friends for advice on retirement planning. Who should you trust the most? The answer to this is easy – yourself of course! Become knowledgeable about your benefits, read through this book for ideas on how to utilize your benefits to the max and don't hesitate to get the help of an expert if needed. Just don't assume that your broker, your insurance agent, or the representative at the bank is that expert, unless you know for certain they have a thorough knowledge of your benefits. Unfortunately, and all too often, I meet with someone who has been given bad advice because their advice giver had no clue how involved their benefits were, many times causing critical financial mistakes that can't be fixed.

HOW TO USE THIS BOOK

The good news is you don't have to read this entire book, or at least not at one sitting. Some of the chapters have relevance to everyone – i.e. Section 2 on the Thrift Savings Plan – while others may not pertain to you at the present time – i.e. Chapter 8 on Social Security. But rest assured, there is definitely something in it for all federal employees. So, read it as you like, but definitely keep it close at hand, because it will prove to be an invaluable guide.

SECTION

CHAPTER
1

CALCULATING YOUR FUTURE –
CSRS AND CSRS OFFSET

———————— ⋆ ————————

As a federal employee, you are a part of the largest workforce in the country, currently about 2.7 million federal workers. You have a complicated set of benefits. You may have started your career under the original retirement system known as the Civil Service Retirement System, or CSRS, which began in 1920. The first person who retired from that system did so in 1926. When they calculated her benefits, they did it with a pencil and paper – and they still calculate your benefits that same way today. The Office of Personnel Management, OPM, has made three attempts at automating the system, but they've never been able to accomplish it. That tells you a little bit about how complicated the benefits are.

If you came to work for the federal government before January 1st of 1984, you are most likely in CSRS, which has its own unique set of characteristics. If you were hired after January 1st of 1984, you were required to pay into Social Security, and a brand-new government pension system was created called the Federal Employees Retirement System or FERS.

CSRS

First, let's talk about the CSRS system. Only 16% of the workforce today is still CSRS, because the rest have all retired. It's predicted that by 2019, all of them will be retired and we'll only have FERS employees left.

In CSRS, two components are used to calculate a pension or annuity (these terms refer to the guaranteed monthly amount you'll receive for the rest of your life). First, you have to be eligible to retire, which is based on the combination of your age and your years of federal service.

To be eligible, you have to be at least 55 years old and must have worked for the government for 30 years. Or, you can be 60 years old and have 20 years of service; or you can be 62 years old and have five years of service.

Most of the people in the two latter groups have already retired, so we're addressing those people who are in their 50s, the majority of whom already have 30 years of service. Once you're at least 55 years old, and have at least 30 years of service, you're in what I call the "Three Bad Days Club," because now you're eligible to retire on an immediate annuity that gets paid out to you on a monthly basis for the rest of your life. We always joke that if you have three bad days in a row at work, you're gone. That's what makes the decision for you.

The Civil Service Retirement System is under attack right now, along with other federal employee benefits. Congress and the general public seem to think that if we just had a smaller government and fewer federal employees, all of our problems would be solved. Of course, when we start to put a pencil to paper we know this isn't true but, as I write this, there's a lot of talk about changing the benefit structures. I can only tell you how it works today, of course, but the threat of those benefits changing is causing federal employees to retire in significantly higher numbers than we've seen in the past few years. In an average year, about 55,000 federal employees retire. That number is up about 22% in 2011.

Once you are eligible to retire, the first question is, "What's the best day to retire? There must be some way that I can figure out how to make the most of my benefits and pick the one best day of the year."

Let me just say that your best day to retire is when you are eligible and you decide you want to go. Beyond that, if you want to utilize sick and annual leave, here's some advice on how best to do just that.

The best day to retire under the Civil Service Retirement System is either on the last day of the month, or in the first three days of a new month. Most CSRS employees choose to retire on the third of the month, because they get paid their salary (which is higher than what their pension will be) through the third, and then they start getting their pensions on the fourth day of the month. They have no unpaid days, and they've maximized their salary. If you can combine that third day of the month with the end of a pay period, you're going to accrue eight more hours of annual leave and four more hours of sick leave.

About 70% of CSRS employees choose to retire at the end of the year, because it's the end of a pay period and also the end of the annual leave year, and you can roll over 240 hours of annual leave. In addition, if you don't take any of your annual leave for your final year of work, you can add 208 hours of accrued leave that you didn't use in that last year before retiring, and get paid out a maximum total of 448 hours of annual leave (240 carryover and 208 maximum one-year annual accrual). That leave gets paid out in the new year, and goes onto the next year's tax return. If there's a cost of living adjustment for that year, you get the COLA on that lump sum annual leave.

The best dates for retirement for 2012 are:
CSRS
February 1, 2 or 3
March 1 or 2
April 2 or 3
May 1, 2 or 3
June 1 (also end of pay period)
July 2 or 3
August 1, 2 or 3
September 3 (also holiday)
October 1, 2 or 3
November 1 or 2 (also end of pay period)
December 3
January 1, 2 or 3, 2013

DOCUMENTS YOU'LL NEED TO HAVE

One of the key things I'd encourage you to do, right now, is to create a "Retirement Documents" file folder. Don't wait until you need them; it's much easier to take care of this now, before you're filling out your retirement paperwork. Here's what you need to have inside your folder:

- A certified copy of your birth certificate. When you go to apply for Medicare, they're going to expect you to prove you're 65, as will Social Security.

- If you were in the military, you'll need your discharge form, the DD214, because you may be able to count the time you served in the military towards your federal service, depending on whether you've made a deposit for this service and when that service occurred.

- A copy of your Social Security statement, which says how many quarters you've worked. You have to go online (www.ssa.gov/estimator) to look at your estimated benefits, and you can print it out from there. The printout does not reflect your Social Security earnings by year, so if you suspect that your estimated benefit is inaccurate, you'll have to schedule an appointment with your local Social Security office to get year-by-year earnings. Look carefully at how many years of earnings you've got, and make sure that your agency didn't under-report them, or make some other error. It's going to be up to you to find mistakes and get them corrected. This is less important for CSRS, because you don't have Social Security as part of the benefits for your federal employment years.

- A copy of your marriage license. The Office of Personnel Management actually requires you to send in a copy of your marriage certificate with your retirement paperwork. This is because some of your former colleagues were trying to give survivor benefits to people they weren't actually married to, so now you have to prove that you're married to the person that you want to receive those benefits.

• If you are divorced, you're also going to want to keep a copy of the divorce decree in this important documents folder, even if your former spouse was not awarded any of your federal benefits. You want to just make sure that you have a copy of it there, so that you can prove that if it comes up.

• The last four documents you'll want to have in your folder are all beneficiary forms. The first one is what happens if you pass away before you actually get to retire; it designates who gets your last paycheck. You probably completed this form early in your career and might not have looked at it since that time. You may not like that person anymore, you may not even be married to that person anymore, so if you aren't sure who you named, now might be a good time to go back and redo the form (SF1152).

• The second form, TSP-3, designates who inherits your TSP if you pass away.

• The third form designates who gets your FEGLI – your group life insurance (SF1153).

• And the final beneficiary form designates who gets your contributions to the retirement system (SF2808). Every pay period, you're making a contribution to the Civil Service Retirement System. If you should pass away before you collect all of those contributions through the retirement benefits, that lump sum of money is inheritable, so you want to make sure you've named a beneficiary.

SF forms can be found at www.opm.gov

Forms for TSP can be found at www.tsp.gov

HOW YOUR ANNUITY WILL BE CALCULATED

Once you know you're eligible to retire, how are they going to calculate your annuity? Your annuity will be calculated on three things; your retirement service computation date, your "high three," and a formula that is based on your years of service.

Let's start with your retirement service computation date. When you look at your leave and earnings statement you'll see a date that says "SCD, service computation date for leave purposes." This means that you may have had the right to accumulate leave at a faster rate based on when you started. Many people assume, "Oh, that's my retirement date. That's the date that they're going use to calculate whether I have 30 years or not." Not necessarily so!

Your retirement service computation date is based on your federal service from the day you were appointed to the day you separated from service, whether you quit or you retired, as long as you were paying into the retirement system. The key point here is that you have to be paying into the system - making contributions. If you started work for the federal government and you were what was called a "co-op" or intern, or you were under temporary service, in all likelihood you were not paying into the retirement system.

While they gave you credit for that time towards accruing leave, it's not creditable for the calculation of your annuity, so we need to make some adjustments for those dates. Your retirement service computation date does include leave without pay up to six months in a calendar year. It includes part-time service, prior to April 7th of 1986. Even if you worked part-time for five years at half time, all five years count. After April 7th of 1986, part-time service counts towards eligibility, but when we calculate your annuity it's going to be prorated. We'll talk about that in more detail in Chapter Three-"A Series of Unique Events."

The retirement service computation date also includes WAE – "when actually employed" time – where 260 days count as a full year for these employees. The only other way to adjust your service computation date for retirement purposes is by paying back a deposit for military time or a redeposit of CSRS contributions that you previously took out. In other words, paying a redeposit if you made contributions to the system, then left the federal government and took out those contributions, and subsequently returned to federal service. You can also add your military time in by paying a deposit. These are the only ways you have to adjust your service computation date.

Your "high three" is one of the federal benefits that has been under attack and review for a number of years. There are people in Washington who think that it should be changed to the "high five," because it would save the government money. It actually used to be the "high five" for CSRS employees, but in the early '70s it was changed to the "high three." While changing it to the "high five" would have something of a negative impact on your annuity, it's not earth-shattering and probably won't amount to more than a few hundred dollars a year.

Your high three is based on your highest three consecutive years of earnings in the federal government. It doesn't have to be three calendar years. It includes base plus locality pay. Nothing else – no cash awards, holiday pay, overtime pay, or military pay – is included in that "high three." It's your base plus locality pay. Once you know your retirement service computation date, you can determine that high three number.

Now, what you really want to figure out is, what's the formula that will be used to calculate your pension? What's the percentage of your "high three" that you're going to use, in order to calculate your estimated annuity?

Creditable Service Worksheet	Year	Month	Day
Creditable Service			
Unused Sick Leave			
Total Creditable Service			

Using this worksheet, start by putting in when you plan to retire. Then, write in your retirement service computation date. Now, we're going do some math. Start on the right hand side and subtract the days. Then, subtract the months. Last, subtract the years. Now you have your years and months of creditable service.

Creditable Service Worksheet	Year	Month	Day
Planned Retirement Date	2013	1	3
Retirement Service Computation Date	1974	6	28
Creditable Service (Line 1 – Line 2)	38	6	5
Unused Sick Leave (use conversion chart)			
Total Creditable Service (Line 3 + Line 4)			

In addition to this, you get to add sick leave. Any hours of unused sick leave that you have at the end of your career, now turn into months, days, and maybe even years, depending on how much you have. Add that to your creditable service for calculation purposes of your annuity.

Creditable Service Worksheet	Year	Month	Day
Planned Retirement Date	2013	1	3
Retirement Service Computation Date	1974	6	28
Creditable Service (Line 1 – Line 2)	38	6	5
Unused Sick Leave (use conversion chart)		6	26
Total Creditable Service (Line 3 + Line 4)	39	1	1

2,081 hours equals one year. If you have more sick leave than that, you subtract 2,081 from the number of hours you have, and you're going have one year, plus the number of months and days left over from that 2,081. In the example above, I used 1,194 hours of sick leave, which equated to 6 months and 26 days.

Sick Leave Chart

# of Days	0 Months +	1 Months +	2 Months +	3 Months +	4 Months +	5 Months +	6 Months +	7 Months +	8 Months +	9 Months +	10 Months +	11 Months +
0	0	174	348	522	696	870	1044	1217	1391	1565	1739	1913
1	6	180	354	528	701	875	1049	1223	1397	1571	1745	1919
2	12	186	359	533	707	881	1055	1229	1403	1577	1751	1925
3	17	191	365	539	713	887	1061	1235	1409	1583	1757	1930
4	23	197	371	545	719	893	1067	1241	1415	1588	1762	1936
5	29	203	377	551	725	899	1072	1246	1420	1594	1768	1942
6	35	209	383	557	730	904	1078	1252	1426	1600	1774	1948
7	41	214	388	562	736	910	1084	1258	1432	1606	1780	1954
8	46	220	394	568	742	916	1090	1264	1438	1612	1786	1959
9	52	226	400	574	748	922	1096	1270	1444	1617	1791	1965
10	58	232	406	580	754	928	1101	1275	1449	1623	1797	1971
11	64	238	412	586	759	933	1107	1281	1455	1629	1803	1977
12	70	243	417	591	765	939	1113	1287	1461	1635	1809	1983
13	75	249	423	597	771	945	1119	1293	1467	1641	1815	1988
14	81	255	429	603	777	951	1125	1299	1472	1646	1820	1994
15	87	261	435	609	783	957	1131	1304	1478	1652	1826	2000
16	93	267	441	615	788	962	1136	1310	1484	1658	1832	2006
17	99	272	446	620	794	968	1142	1316	1490	1664	1838	2012
18	104	278	452	626	800	974	1148	1322	1496	1670	1844	2017
19	110	284	458	632	806	980	1154	1328	1501	1675	1849	2023
20	116	290	464	638	812	986	1159	1333	1507	1681	1855	2029
21	122	296	470	643	817	991	1165	1339	1513	1687	1861	2035
22	128	301	475	649	823	997	1171	1345	1519	1693	1867	2041
23	133	307	481	655	829	1003	1177	1351	1525	1699	1873	2046
24	139	313	487	661	835	1009	1183	1357	1530	1704	1878	2052
25	145	319	493	667	841	1015	1189	1362	1536	1710	1884	2058
26	151	325	499	672	846	1020	1194	1368	1542	1716	1890	2064
27	157	330	504	678	852	1026	1200	1374	1548	1722	1896	2070
28	162	336	510	684	858	1032	1206	1380	1554	1728	1902	2075
29	168	342	516	690	864	1038	1212	1386	1559	1733	1907	2081

★ ★

What's the most sick leave I've ever heard of anyone accumulating? There's a gentleman who just celebrated his 86th birthday, who started to work for the federal government in 1948. This fall, he will have 63 years of federal service, and he has over 6,000 hours of sick leave! The people who've talked to me about him say, "Oh, he'll never retire." He's something of a legend in his own agency and they also report that he's very, very sharp. Granted, he's an extreme example, but many people under CSRS have more than a year of sick leave.

★ ★

If you're like most CSRS employees, you always saved your sick leave, and didn't use it if you didn't have to. Now you get to use it! Add your sick leave days to any days you had left over from that initial calculation, and if it equals 30 days, you get to add another month to your creditable service. If it doesn't add up to a month you get to contract something known as the "CSRS flu," which means that you're going try to use up those days before you retire. You want to calculate this very carefully.

Now you know how many years and how many months of service you're going to have your benefits calculated on. The easiest way to get your formula is to take those years and months and turn them into a decimal. Let's say you have exactly 34 years of service. You're going to subtract two, then multiply it by 2, and you're going to add .25%.

For that person with 34 years of service, when we subtract two we get 32. When we multiply that by two, we get 64, and then we add .25%. By these calculations, your annuity will be based on 64.25% of your "high three." If you had 34½ years, we'd do 34.5 minus two, times two, plus the .25%. That's the easiest way to get the formula that you're going to use to determine what your annual annuity is going to be.

Once we know what your annual annuity is going to be, we can divide that number by 12, which tells us what your gross monthly annuity will be. This is before taxes, before insurance and, if you're married, before we take out for survivor benefits. (Keep in mind if there's any change after we divide by 12, OPM "keeps the change.")

It's important for you to understand the moving parts of how OPM calculates your annuity, because you're going to get an estimate from your HR department before you retire. You may decide to work with a financial advisor, and he or she might give you an estimate as well. If OPM sends you something different than what you've calculated, you want to be able to say, "Wait a minute. I recognize that this isn't right because I know how it should have been calculated." That's the main reason you want to understand these moving parts and exactly what goes into calculating a federal pension.

For CSRS, we've covered how we're going to calculate your annuity, and what the best day to retire is. We've talked about your sick leave and managing that sick leave. Keep in mind: You want to make sure that you don't look at your sick leave in isolation. In other words, when you've calculated those hours and you see how many months and days you're going to have, you don't want to just look at that number and say, "Oh, I'm going to have six months and 26 days, so I'm going to use my 26 days of sick leave up and just count the six months toward my annuity," because we know that if you had at least four days left over from your creditable service, it would count as another month when added to that 26 days. That's why we say don't look at those sick leave hours by themselves. You want to add them to your actual creditable service before you determine just exactly how long you're going be "in quarantine" before retirement.

MILITARY SERVICE AND CSRS

Under the CSRS system, if you are retired military and you're receiving military pay, it makes no sense for you to stop taking that wonderful military benefit in order to buy back that time to have it count under CSRS. You're going want to keep receiving that military retirement pay.

If you have military service before October 1, 1982, you are allowed to count your military time toward your CSRS service for retirement purposes without paying a deposit for that service. However, if you are eligible for Social Security at age 62, your CSRS annuity will be re-calculated without that military service, and you will receive a lower CSRS annuity at that time. This provision is known as "Catch-62."

The key here is to understand whether you are eligible for Social Security at age 62 or are likely to become eligible by age 62. Then you can determine whether to pay back your military time. The majority of the CSRS employees won't be eligible for Social Security at age 62, and they have nothing to worry about. They don't have to make the deposit, and they do get to count it.

If you have military service after October 1, 1982 that you want to buy back, you're going to pay 7% of your military pay at that time. Were you highly compensated if you were in the military sometime in the late '70s or early '80s? Probably not, so 7% of that number isn't going to amount to a lot of money. However, the interest that they're going to charge you on that is going to be worse than the cost of making the deposit itself. That said, it will most likely still make sense for you to make that deposit, because if you pay that time back you're going to get to count it all.

You're going to get to count that time towards the calculation of your annuity, and you're going to get paid out that benefit for the rest of your life. If you have not paid it back yet and you're trying to determine whether or not it makes sense to pay back this military deposit, have your HR department or your financial advisor run your estimates both ways, and see what the monthly difference is between the two, then divide that into what the cost would be to make your military deposit. That's going to give you the number of months it would take you to recover that amount. If it's less than 10 years, and you think you're going to live longer than 10 years, it probably makes sense to go ahead and pay it back. If it looks like it would take you longer than 10 years to recoup it, then you may have to think long and hard about whether you actually want to make that payment.

HOW TO PROVIDE FOR YOUR SURVIVORS

The best benefit that you get for having been a federal employee all these years is your pension. And you get that pension for life, a benefit that has all but disappeared in the private sector, where even career employees are cut loose after thirty-year careers with nothing but a handshake.

The second-best benefit that you get is receiving your health benefits for the rest of your life, with the federal government picking up 72% of your premium. The 28% you are responsible for is the same percentage you pay today. If you elect a survivor benefit for your spouse, you not only get to keep those health benefits for life, but so does your spouse.

You get access to the same health benefits you've had, and you get to access open season, which we'll talk about in the FEHB chapter. You can change your plan each and every year, and additionally you get some very special choices and options with Medicare that no other group receives. If you don't remember anything else from this chapter, and you're married, the one thing you want to take away is the importance of electing a survivor benefit for your spouse to allow you both to hang onto health benefits, with the federal government continuing to pay a significant portion of the premium. Even if you, as the federal employee, choose to leave your spouse as little as one dollar of survivor benefits, your spouse still gets to keep your health benefits in the event of your passing away first.

Of course, most federal employees don't leave their spouses with just a dollar. You can leave them a maximum benefit, which is 55%. In order to leave your spouse 55%, it's going cost you roughly 10% of your annuity. (The actual formula is 2.5% of the first $3,600 of your annual computed annuity plus 10% of any amount over that $3,600). You can opt to leave them anything between one dollar and the 55%. If you decide, "Oh, my spouse doesn't really need the financial support of the survivor benefit, but they really do need the health insurance," you could calculate the survivor benefit so it leaves your surviving spouse enough benefits to pay the health insurance premium. You'll want to consider the highest premium in OPM for a single person and leave your spouse something roughly 50% higher to pay those premiums, because we know that the cost of healthcare is rising faster than the cost of living adjustments you get on your pension.

For example, if your share of the current highest premium for health benefits in your state (if that's where you plan to retire) is $200, you would add 50% to that amount. You would want to provide $300 a month, or $3,600 a year, to your surviving spouse. The actual calculation on your retirement paperwork is confusing on this topic, because it asks you to calculate 55% of what number you want to leave your survivor. Huh? The easiest way to get this number is to divide the annual amount you want to leave for your survivor by 55%. This will provide the number you'll write on your retirement paperwork.

You can leave survivor benefits to your current spouse. Much to your current spouse's surprise, you may also leave it to a former spouse if ordered to by a court. You can leave it to an insurable interest, which is someone who is closer to you than a first cousin and who is financially dependent upon you. This may be someone like your parents who are now financially dependent upon you. It is not your 32-year-old child who simply doesn't want to work for a living. Minor children are also covered up to the age of 18, and you don't pay anything extra for that. It's very generous of OPM to give you that benefit, but keep in mind that your minor children aren't going to be minor forever.

Another strategy which married CSRS employees use to cover the survivorship benefit is to use life insurance instead of the survivor benefit. We know that the cost of the survivor benefit goes up each year, every time the federal employee gets a cost of living adjustment on their pension. You might pay into that survivor benefit for 20 or 25 years. At that point, you might have paid in $100,000 or $150,000, but what happens if your spouse passes away first? That's right – OPM wins. They keep that lump sum. You no longer have to pay into that survivor benefit, but you do have to give up all the money that you've paid in up to that point.

So, many people decide, "I'm going leave my spouse just enough of a survivor benefit to cover the health insurance premiums, and I'm going to take the difference of what I would have spent in the annuity and get some life insurance on myself. That way if my spouse passes away first, I can name another beneficiary."

Year	Age	Monthly Annuity w/out Survivor	Monthly Annuity with Survivor	Survivor's Monthly Benefit	Survivor Benefit Cost	Annual Difference	Accum. Annual Diff.
1	55	3,928	3,559	2,161	370	4,445	4,446
20	75	6,862	6,240	3,789	649	7,794	119,427

This example illustrates how both the survivor benefit and the cost of the survivor benefit increase as the retiree receives COLA's each year. In 20 years, the cost would be nearly $120,000!

Year	Age	Monthly Annuity w/out Survivor	Monthly Annuity with Survivor	Survivor's Monthly Benefit	Survivor Benefit Cost	Annual Difference	Accum. Annual Diff.
1	55	3,928	3,903	259	25	300	300
20	75	6,862	6,821	425	41	492	8,044

By reducing the amount of the survivor benefit, the cost is reduced as well. The difference can then be used to purchase permanent life insurance coverage. Keep in mind that this strategy does not work in all cases, and it is important to analyze all factors, including the federal employee's health (ability to get life insurance coverage), age, amount of life insurance coverage available, and ability of the surviving spouse to manage the life insurance proceeds.

HOW DOES SOCIAL SECURITY AFFECT THE CSRS ANNUITY?

Let's start by talking about those of you who fall into the category of CSRS Offset, which is that unique scenario in which you've worked for the federal government, put in at least five years of service, then left the federal government prior to 1984, and subsequently returned to work for the government after at least a one-year break in service.

If you returned to work after January 1st of 1984, remember that Congress said anybody hired in the federal government after January 1, 1984 was required to pay into Social Security. If you come back and want to be in the Civil Service Retirement System, you are required to pay into Social Security. Consequently, you become part of a hybrid system known as the CSRS Offset, and you pay into both the CSRS system and Social Security.

If you are eligible for a pension based on employment that did not require you to pay into Social Security (i.e., CSRS), but you're still eligible for Social Security benefits, Social Security says, "Wait a minute." It's going to look like you are a low-wage earner and you're going get a higher benefit than you're really entitled to.

Social Security will apply something known as the Windfall Elimination Provision (WEP), which means that if you are eligible for Social Security and a CSRS pension, they are going to subtract something from your benefit. The amount that will be subtracted is based on how many years of substantial earnings you have under the Social Security system. If you want to know which years will count as substantial earnings years, you can get out your Social Security Statement, then go to the SSA website page: http://www.ssa.gov/pubs/10045.html#amount.

Look at page three of your Social Security statement, where it lists all of your earnings over your lifetime, compare that with the years/earnings list you'll find on the Social Security website, and check off those years in which your earnings count as substantial earnings. If you can get to 30 years of substantial earnings during which you were paying into Social Security, you're not subject to the Windfall Elimination Provision. Most CSRS employees can't meet that benchmark because they paid into Social Security for less than 30 years. They might have paid in when they were in college, or maybe they worked a part-time job. If you have anything less than 30 years, your Social Security benefit will be reduced by an amount that is based on that number of years. If you have less than 20 years of substantial earnings, the maximum reduction taken for the WEP in 2011 is $381. If you have more than 20, but not 30, the deduction will come down year by year, based on that $381. But the maximum amount your Social Security can be reduced is $381.

Now you may be thinking, "I'm not going to collect much, if anything, on my own Social Security benefit. But if my spouse is eligible for Social Security, while they're still alive I can collect half of their benefit. I think I'll just do that; I'll collect my nice CSRS pension, half my spouse's Social Security, and life should be pretty good in retirement."

Well, Congress is onto you again, and in 1986 they passed a provision known as the Government Pension Offset. If you have a government pension where you did not pay into Social Security, you may be eligible for a portion of your spouse's benefit. Here's how that amount will be determined.

Start with the benefit that you're eligible for from your spouse – half of your spouse's benefit – and subtract two-thirds of your pension. If there's anything left, you can have it. The only good news is that if it's a negative number they don't ask you to pay them!

THE VOLUNTARY CONTRIBUTION PROGRAM

The Voluntary Contribution Program ("VCP") is the best benefit for CSRS and CSRS Offset that most remaining employees have never heard of. It is something of a relic; it was created as a result of federal employees going to OPM and saying, "We contribute 7% of every paycheck to our retirement system, but we'd like the opportunity to be able to contribute even more of that, so that at the end of our careers, it would increase the amount of our annuity." A very popular way to do this at the time was a structure created for both municipal and state governments, which the federal government decided to utilize - the Voluntary Contribution Program.

The program was designed to put after-tax dollars into their retirement system. It earns a fixed interest rate declared by the Treasury Department each year. The funds grow tax-deferred, and when you retire, add an additional benefit to your pension. In 1987, the Thrift Savings Plan was created and, at that point, the Voluntary Contribution Program went to the federal government's deepest, darkest storeroom. And it wasn't thought about again for almost 20 years, because if you had access to the TSP where you can control how the funds are invested, you had more opportunity, so it made more sense to use the TSP.

In 2006, Congress passed the Pension Protection Act of 2006 and a congressman with a horse in the race at the very last moment added an earmark that said, "If you have a Voluntary Contribution Program, when you roll those funds out you can put them in a Roth IRA." Well, all of a sudden they had our attention! It was like, "Wow! You mean to tell me that I can make these contributions with after-tax dollars and earn interest on them, and then get a large chunk of money in a Roth IRA at the end of my career? That is a great deal."

CSRS and CSRS Offsets are eligible to contribute 10% of everything they made as a federal employee, so the amounts that can be contributed often range anywhere from $125,000 to $250,000. When you consider that the amount you can contribute to a traditional Roth IRA each year is $5,000, or $6,000 if you happen to be age 50 or older, this is a huge windfall for CSRS employees. It provides the opportunity to get significant amounts of assets into a Roth IRA right at the end of their careers.

Some rules you'll need to know include: You cannot owe a deposit or a redeposit. If you owe those, you have to pay them back before you can contribute. You're going to apply for a VCP account number using SF-2804. It is the shortest government form you're ever going to fill out and the easiest. You answer three simple questions – do you owe a deposit? Do you owe a redeposit? Have you ever participated in the VCP before? Then you're going to have HR sign off on the form, and you send it off to OPM (the address is included on the form). In 10 to 14 days, you'll get back a VCP account number, and you can start making contributions.

You can put in as little or as much as you want up to your maximum level. It has to be contributed in $25 increments. In other words, you can't send them $472.16. It has to be divisible by $25. You can send in as many deposits as you want. Once you have it fully funded, even if you're still working, you can transfer those funds right back out to a Roth IRA. Any interest that you earn will be taxable. You'll pay the taxes on those earnings, and then the entire amount will be a Roth IRA and will grow tax free for the remainder of your life.

Earnings may be withdrawn tax and penalty free after the 5-year period, if you are 59 ½ (or other qualifying conditions) are also met.

CHAPTER
2

CALCULATING YOUR FUTURE –
FERS/FERS TRANSFEREES

T he FERS Retirement System was created early in the 1980s for federal employees, which were the largest group of employees in our country at the time. Prior to the creation of FERS, federal employees didn't pay into Social Security. Congress looked around and said, "Okay, we think Social Security might be in trouble. You know what we should do? We should get those federal employees to pay into Social Security." Thus, the new Federal Employee Retirement System was born.

Anyone hired after January 1, 1984, who did not have at least 5 years of service by January 1, 1987, is required to pay into Social Security and the Federal Employee Retirement System. Those who were hired after January 1 of 1987 normally contribute 7% of their pay to their retirement; 6.2% goes to Social Security, and 0.8% to FERS. We have seen in the past year where they've actually reduced the Social Security contribution to 4.2%, but you're still going to contribute 0.8% to the FERS Retirement System.

A hybrid of the FERS system includes those people who were in CSRS at one time and opted to go into FERS on their own accord. We know that anyone who was hired after January 1, 1984, who didn't have at least 5 years of federal employment on January 1, 1987, automatically had to go into FERS. However, employees who had at least five years of CSRS employment were offered the opportunity to go to this new retirement system three times; in 1987, 1988, and 1998. That's one way you could become a FERS Transferee. Their annuity is calculated as if they were CSRS employees for their CSRS years, then all the years after they become a FERS Transferee are calculated under FERS.

The other way to become a FERS Transferee is to have worked for the federal government and had at least five years of service under CSRS or as a CSRS Offset, and then left federal service. If you came back after one year or more, you could choose to go into the FERS system. One of the benefits offered to get you to come into FERS was portability. If you thought you weren't going to stay with the federal government, then FERS was more portable. A third of a FERS retiree's income in retirement is designed to come from the Thrift Savings Plan, and that Thrift Savings Plan is portable. The larger annuity that the CSRS offers is not portable. You can't take it with you to another job; you have to wait until you're old enough to actually receive the benefit.

HOW AND WHEN DO I QUALIFY
FOR MY ANNUITY?

In order to retire on an immediate, unreduced annuity, a FERS employee has to meet certain criteria: You have to reach a certain age, and you have to have a certain number of years of service in order to qualify.

If you were born	Your FERS MRA is:
before 1948	55
in 1948	55 and 2 months
in 1949	55 and 4 months
in 1950	55 and 6 months
in 1951	55 and 8 months
in 1952	55 and 10 months
in 1953 – 1964	56
in 1965	56 and 2 months
in 1966	56 and 4 months
in 1967	56 and 6 months
in 1968	56 and 8 months
in 1969	56 and 10 months
1970 or after	57

You must have reached your MRA and have 30 years of service; or you can be 60 years old and have 20 years of service; or you can be 62 years old with only 5 years of service and be eligible to retire on an immediate, unreduced annuity. We're seeing more and more people come to the federal government at the end of their careers in order to work the last five to ten years within the federal government. The biggest benefit for doing this is that they get to take their health care benefits with them into retirement.

Under FERS, you have the option to take a voluntary early out. This means that if you attain your MRA and you have as little as ten years of service, you can retire on an immediate annuity; however, your benefit is reduced by 5/12 of 1 percent for each month that you're under age 62. An easier way to think of this is that it's 5% a year. For example, let's say that you reach your MRA of 57, you have at least 10 years of service, and you want to retire. You don't want to wait until you're 60; you don't want to wait until you're 62. You can retire on an immediate annuity; however, there's going to be a penalty deducted from it of 5% for every year that you're under age 62. A 57-year-old would be 5 years under age 62; they would take a 25% penalty against their annuity, and that penalty is permanent. It doesn't end when they turn 62. But it is a way for people who want to leave the federal government early and take an immediate annuity to do that.

One exception to this is if you are retiring on your MRA with ten years of service and you say, "I don't really want to pay that penalty, and I could live without my annuity for a few years. I plan to go get another job somewhere else anyway." You could actually defer taking your annuity until you are age 60, if you have at least 20 years of service, or age 62 if you have less than 20 years of service when you leave. You can receive your annuity at that point without the penalty.

You might also be offered an involuntary early out that would allow you to take an immediate annuity without any reduction. You're eligible to take this "early out" offer at age 50 with 20 years of service, or any age with 25 years of service. These offers are called VERAs, which is where your agency goes to OPM and petitions them for a Voluntary Early Reduction Authority. The agency has to get OPM's approval to reduce their workforce. The agency determines which jobs and which functions it could do without, and then makes that early out offer to you. If you are 50 years old with 20 years of service or any age with 25 years of service, you're allowed to retire on an immediate annuity and avoid the reduction.

Depending on the composition of the agency workforce, offering a VERA may not get the desired number of volunteers for the early out. It may become necessary for the agency to go back to OPM and ask for permission to offer a Voluntary Separation Incentive Payment, or VSIP, to their employees to "sweeten the pot." You'll also hear these payments referred to as buyouts, and they usually amount to $25,000. Some agencies offer less, but at this time it cannot be more than $25,000.

WHAT ARE THE BEST DATES TO RETIRE?

That's a question we hear quite commonly. Of course, the best date to retire is when you become eligible and you decide you're ready. But in addition to that, we can line up certain things to make sure that you maximize the value of your benefits.

For a FERS employee, retiring on the last day of the month allows you to make the most of your benefits. You're paid through that last day of the month and your annuity begins on the first day of the following month, so you don't have any days that are unpaid. If you can combine that last day of the month with the end of a pay period, then you will accrue four hours of sick leave and eight hours of annual leave for that pay period. In the grand scheme of things, this is not going to make or break your retirement, but if you can make sure that all those pieces line up, it's just one more little added benefit.

Most federal employees, about 70 percent, retire on the last day of the year, because they are allowed to roll over their maximum annual leave at that point. Each year, you can carry over 240 hours of annual leave. If you do not take any leave during your final year of employment, you will accrue another 208 hours, so if you retire on the last day of the year, you are going to be paid for 448 hours of annual leave at your hourly rate. You're going to receive a cost of living adjustment on that leave if there's a cost of living that year, and you get to pay your taxes in the new year. That lump sum doesn't go on top of a full year's salary; it gets combined with your pension in the following year and could cause you to have a lower effective tax rate.

The best dates for retirement for 2012 are:

FERS

January 31

February 29

March 31

April 30

May 31 (holiday!)

June 30 (also end of pay period)

July 31

August 31

September 30

October 31

November 30

December 31

CALCULATING YOUR ANNUITY

Once you become eligible and you've determined the best date, you next want to calculate your federal annuity. It's based on three things; your years of service based on your retirement service computation date, your "high three" salary, and a formula.

Your retirement service computation date is based on the time between when you were hired and when you separate, as long as retirement deductions were being withheld. As long as that 0.8% that goes into FERS is being withheld, the time counts. It includes up to six months of leave without pay in a calendar year; it includes all part-time service prior to April 7, 1986. If you have part-time service on or after April 7, 1986, it includes credit for the eligibility in order to qualify to calculate your annuity, but when the annuity is actually calculated, that time is going to be prorated. As an example, if you worked 5 years at 50% time, it's going to be prorated, and the amount used to calculate your annuity would only be 2½ years. Intermittent days' work also count toward your service computation date, and as we'll talk about in "A Series of Unique Events," the only other way to add to your service time is by paying back for military service, making a deposit for service where your retirement contributions were not withheld, or making a redeposit.

Annual leave for FERS employees is based on how many years of service you have.

Employee Type	Less than 3 years of service*	3 years but less than 15 years of service*	15 or more years of service*
Full time employees	1/2 day (4 hours) for each pay period	3/4 day (6 hours) for each pay period, except 1 1/4 day (10 hours) in last pay period	1 day (8 hours) for each pay period
Part time employees**	1 hour of annual leave for each 20 hours in a pay status	1 hour of annual leave for each 13 hours in a pay status	1 hour of annual leave for each 10 hours in a pay status

Full-time employees with less than 3 years of service earn 4 hours, or a half a day, of leave for each pay period. If you have 3 years of service but less than 15, that bumps up to ¾ of a day, or 6 hours for each pay period, except you get a day and a quarter for the last pay period. And finally, once you have 15 years of federal service, you are going to get 8 hours of accrued annual leave for each and every pay period, or 208 hours per year. Part-time employees with less than 3 years of service accrue 1 hour of annual leave for each 20 hours in pay status. When they reach that 3-year anniversary, they receive 1 hour of annual leave for every 13 hours in pay status, and finally, once they have over 15 years of service, they receive 1 hour of annual leave for every 10 hours in pay status. They are allowed to carry over 240 hours of annual leave each year. If you have any more than 240 hours, it's known as "use or lose." At the end your career, you're paid out for unused annual leave.

Sick leave is not based on your years of service; you simply accrue 4 hours of sick leave for every pay period. Prior to January 1, 2014, FERS employees who are ready to retire will be allowed to add 50 percent of their sick leave to their creditable service for the calculation of their annuity. After January 1, 2014, FERS retirees will be allowed to count all of their sick leave. If you're considering retiring in the middle of 2013 versus the end of the year, depending on how much sick leave you have, this might be a determining factor.

Your "high three" salary is the next component that we need to know in order to calculate your FERS annuity. The high three average is the average of your base plus locality pay, over any three consecutive years of creditable service. It does not include anything other than base plus locality pay; no bonuses, no holiday pay, overtime pay, military pay, travel or cash awards. It's simply your base plus locality pay over any three consecutive years. Typically, it is your last three years of service, but it doesn't have to be.

And finally, you're going to apply a formula to that high three average in order to come up with your annual annuity. You receive 1% for each year of service, multiplied by your high three. If you work for 30 years, you're going to get 30% of your high three. If you work for 25 years, you're going to get 25% of your high three. If you work until you are 62 and you have at least 20 years of service, you'll receive a 10% bonus on your annuity. You get to use 1.1% times each of those years of service, instead of 1%. Using the numbers from the previous example, if you were 62 years old when you retired with 30 years of service, you would get 33% of your high three as opposed to 30 percent, which is a 10% boost.

SURVIVOR BENEFITS

There are two survivor benefits available to FERS retirees. If you are married, you can provide your spouse with either a 25% benefit or a 50% benefit. The cost for the 25% benefit is 5 percent of your annuity, and for the 50% benefit, it's 10 percent of your annuity. This survivor benefit is available to your current spouse; much to your current spouse's surprise, it is also available to a former spouse if it was indicated in the divorce decree or by court order. It is available to an insurable interest, which is someone who is closer to you than a first cousin who is financially dependent upon you (for instance, a special needs child); and it is available to your minor children.

A key point on survivor benefits is that the retiree must elect at least a minimum survivor benefit for his spouse, in order for his spouse to continue receiving health benefits if the employee passes away first. One of the great benefits that you have in addition to your pension is the fact that you get to continue your health benefits into retirement for both you and your spouse as long as you're both alive, with the federal government paying 72% of the premium and you paying 28% of the premium. This occurs as long as you make sure to keep that survivor benefit for your spouse.

One of the things that concerns federal employees is the feeling that they might not even make it to retirement. What happens if you die at your desk? (Sometimes it feels like that, doesn't it?)

With at least 18 months of creditable service, but prior to retirement, your survivor would receive a lump sum benefit of $29,722, which is adjusted annually for inflation, plus half of the greater of your high three average or your current salary. Additionally, with at least 10 years of creditable service, your surviving spouse would receive not only the lump sum benefit from above, but also 50% of your annuity calculated as of the date of your death. It would be presumed that you would have elected the 50% survivor benefit for your spouse, and they would automatically get 50% of your annuity. If they were on your health insurance, they would automatically continue with those health benefits as well. Any Social Security or other survivor benefits are not affected by these lump sum payments.

DISABILITY

There are many great benefits for FERS, but one thing that is missing from the plan is either short-term or long-term disability insurance. Sick leave acts as a short-term disability policy; the only alternative for long-term disability is a disability retirement. It's available if you are no longer able to do your job in your current position, and you are not qualified for any other position in the same location at the same grade and pay.

Disability retirement doesn't mean that you can't work; you are allowed to get another job and still receive a disability retirement. If you are eligible for a disability retirement, you may make up to 80% of your federal pay in a private sector job. You will continue your health and life insurance coverage as long as you were previously insured for the 5 years before you apply for the disability retirement.

You must have worked for the federal government for at least 18 months, and you have to apply for benefits. If you are incapacitated and not capable of applying for yourself, then your agency, a guardian, or another interested person can apply for you. You must also apply for Social Security disability benefits. It does not mean that you must be awarded Social Security disability benefits, but you must at least apply. And if you meet those requirements, and are approved, your benefits will be calculated as follows.

The first year, you will get 60% of your high three, less any benefits you may be awarded from Social Security. These benefits are taxable. After that first year and beyond, you're going to get 40% of your high three, less 60% of any benefits that you receive from Social Security.

Social Security disability benefits are fairly hard to qualify for; the requirements are stringent, so it's likely that in that first year, you may not be receiving Social Security benefits. You may have to wait until the end of that second or third year for Social Security disability to finally kick in. At age 62, your disability benefit will be re-calculated as if you had worked all those years up to age 62, and then it will be calculated just as a regular FERS annuity would be calculated. Of course, your high three from when you first qualified for the disability retirement will be used in that re-calculation.

SOCIAL SECURITY AND THE FERS RETIREE

The FERS system has three parts: the FERS annuity, which we've just talked about, Social Security, and the Thrift Savings Plan. The earliest age that Social Security is available is age 62, but when we looked at the eligibility to retire, we saw that many FERS employees have an MRA (Minimum Retirement Age) of 55, 56, and no higher than 57. Yet at that point you wouldn't be eligible for Social Security, so OPM came up with what's known as the FERS supplement.

If you retire at your MRA and have 30 years of service, or you retire at age 60 with 20 years of service, you are eligible for this payment, which comes directly from OPM into your bank account to supplement your pension until you are eligible for Social Security. If you choose not to take Social Security at age 62, OPM doesn't keep paying you. They stop your benefits at age 62, whether or not you take Social Security. Your FERS supplement is calculated based on your years of FERS service divided by 40. This is actual FERS service – so if you've purchased military time, it's going be subtracted before dividing by 40. That's going to give you a fraction that will be multiplied times the Social Security benefit that is projected for you at age 62. You can find this estimate by going to http://www.ssa.gov/estimator and putting in your information. It will pull up your Social Security record and tell you what your age 62 benefit will be. If you have 30 years of creditable service you would divide 30 by 40, which would give you 30/40, or 75% of that Social Security benefit.

While you are earning this FERS supplement, it has the same earnings limitations as when you take Social Security at age 62. This means that if you think you're going to go out and get the "fun" job when you retire and collect your pension and collect your Social

Security supplement and take money from your TSP – well, that fun job better not pay very well, because your FERS supplement is subject to the Social Security earnings test, which for 2012 is $14,660. If you earn more than $14,660, for every $2.00 over that that you earn, you will give $1.00 back out of your Social Security or your FERS supplement.

Social Security benefits are covered extensively in the Social Security chapter. Every few years a rumor spreads through federal agencies that FERS retirees aren't entitled to full Social Security benefits and that you are subject to something called the Windfall Elimination Provision ("WEP"). Unless you are a FERS Transferee, you will not be covered under the WEP.

You do not have to worry about not being able to collect your Social Security benefits. There are three components for the FERS retiree: their pension, Social Security, and the TSP. The WEP does NOT apply to retirees who earn a pension where they paid into Social Security, which FERS retirees did.

In retirement, you will receive cost of living adjustments based on a percentage of the Consumer Price Index for urban and clerical wage earners (CPI-W). If the CPI-W measured as of September 30 is between 0 and 2 percent, the FERS retiree gets all of that increase awarded on December 1 and it shows up on his January 1st annuity payment. If the CPI-W is between two and three percent, FERS retirees get a flat two percent, and a CPI-W anywhere over three percent provides the CPI minus one percent as their cost of living increase.

The first year after retirement, if you retire in the middle of the year, your Cost Of Living Adjustment ("COLA") will be prorated. The most important thing for the FERS retiree to remember is that you will NOT receive your first COLA until you reach age 62. This can be an important thing to consider if you are retiring at your MRA of, say, 56 years old, and we have a burst of inflation in our economy of, say, 3% a year. Between 56 and 62, you would have 6 years, or 18%, that your pension would have fallen behind the actual economy until you get your first COLA. It is even more important when you consider that for many people going into retirement in the near future, you may not have gotten any cost of living increases during your final working years. Your salary may have been frozen for a few years, and that combined with the lack of a retirement COLA until age 62 can have a big effect on your overall retirement income.

CHAPTER 3

A SERIES OF UNIQUE EVENTS– PART-TIME, DEPOSITS AND OFFSETS – OH MY!

---- ★ ----

As Chris laid out her paperwork on the desk, it seemed like one of those magic tricks where the hankies just keep coming out of a small object. With seven different periods of part-time service at three different agencies (all at different hours per pay period), a break in service (where she'd withdrawn her retirement contributions), and military service (for which she had not made a deposit), no one had ever been able to provide a reasonable estimate of her retirement benefits.

Even seasoned benefits officers can be challenged when one employee has such a complicated record. It was important for Chris to understand the components involved in calculating each of her "unique events." All of these events are allowed for federal workers- it's how they affect your overall retirement that can be overwhelming.

After some education on part-time service and its effect on retirement, what it means to be a CSRS Offset (and why you always hear it's the best of all systems), and a plan for repaying her military deposit, Chris left feeling in control of her federal service. Knowledge is power!

Covered in this chapter will be all those things that can put a little twist on the calculation of your benefits. We'll talk about deposits and redeposits, buying back military time, and part-time service, and how these unique events might affect the calculation of your annuity.

The definition of a deposit is when an employee has had a period or periods of service where he or she did not contribute into his or her retirement, either CSRS or FERS. This may include seasonal time or co-op time; you may have been an intern. You came to work for the government, you were paid by the government, but you weren't a full-time or a career-conditional employee, and so they weren't withholding retirement deductions because it wasn't clear you were going to stay with the government.

If you later became a full-time employee, you may want to count that time towards the calculation of your annuity and certainly towards being eligible. Under the CSRS system, if you have service prior to October 1, 1982, and you have not made a deposit for that time, 100% of it counts towards the eligibility. However, your annuity will be reduced by 10% of the deposit owed that you should have paid back. Keep in mind that it's not just the amount of the deposit but the amount of the accrued interest, together with the amount of that deposit, that you'll need to consider when determining whether to pay it. The longer you wait to pay it back, the larger that sum becomes.

Deposits almost always occur from time worked at the beginning of your career, and sometimes you don't think about paying it back until near the end of your career, when interest has accrued and can make a pretty large difference in the amount that you owe. If you make the deposit, of course, you get to count it for eligibility and the annuity computation in all cases.

In the CSRS System, if you have service prior to October 1, 1982, and you make the deposit; it all counts. If the deposit is not made, you get to count 100% of the time for eligibility, and the annuity is reduced by 10% of the deposit due. If you have service after October 1, 1982, and you make the deposit, you get 100% for eligibility and annuity computation. If you do not make the deposit, you get to count the time for being eligible but get no credit for your annuity computation.

In the FERS System, if you have service prior to January 1, 1989, and make the deposit, you're going to get to count it. If you do not make the deposit, you get no credit for eligibility or the annuity computation. That's a significant point for FERS employees who have any non-creditable, non-deposit service prior to January 1, 1989. In most cases, they're going to want to make that deposit because they're going to want to get to count the time both for eligibility and the calculation of their annuity. For FERS, if a deposit is owed for any service after January 1, 1989, you aren't even given the option to make a deposit. It's not allowed.

What are the pros and cons? Should you make that deposit? Under CSRS, for that initial deposit for the service prior to October 1, 1982, a general rule of thumb is that it often makes sense to make the deposit. If your deposit isn't made, your annuity is reduced by 10% of the amount due, and conventional wisdom would dictate that if you think you're going live longer than 10 years in retirement, you'd repay the deposit, because even though it's reduced by 10%, and presumably in 10 years your deposit would be repaid, they continue to take that deduction long after the 10 years are up. So if you think you're going to live longer than 10 years and you want to bet on yourself, you may want to repay that deposit plus interest.

For service after October 1, 1982, for a CSRS employee, if the deposit isn't made, you don't get any credit for the annuity computation, and you're going to want to have the calculation run on your pension both with and without the deposit. Divide the difference between those two options into how much you owe to determine how many months it would take to recover the deposit. Again, if it will take you less than 10 years to recover it, you might want to consider repaying it. In most instances, the redeposit amount (original amount plus interest) will be so high that you won't want to repay it, but there are cases where you will, so you want to run the numbers to be sure.

Under FERS for the service prior to January 1, 1989, you're going to do the same thing I just described for CSRS. You're going to run the annuity calculation, both with and without the deposit, take the difference between the two, and divide it into the overall deposit amount plus interest that's owed to get the number of months it would take to recover that deposit. Then make the determination whether you think you're going to live longer than that, and act accordingly.

On redeposits, this applies to an employee who worked for the federal government and paid into the retirement system, then left federal service. When employees leave federal service, they all say the same thing: "I'm never coming back." And they take a refund of their contributions – that 0.8% that they contribute to FERS or the

7% that they contribute to CSRS – and they say, "That was all my money. I put it in the system. I would like it all back, please."

Well, many of them did what they said they were never going do; they came back to work for the government. They found out that the grass wasn't necessarily greener on the private sector side of the street, and they come back to work for the government. If they want their prior time to count, they have to repay what they took out – make a redeposit – in order for it to count for their eligibility and the calculation of their annuity.

In all cases, if you left federal service and you did not take your contributions out and they were not refunded, you don't have anything to worry about. They're still sitting there with your name on them, just waiting for you to come back to work for the federal government. You don't need to do anything.

If your contributions were refunded for service ended before October 1, 1990, and a redeposit is not made, under the CSRS system, you get to count all the time for the eligibility, but your annuity will be actuarially reduced. What that means is the guys with the little green eye shades will try to calculate how long they think you're going to live, and based on that number of years, they're going to reduce your annuity accordingly. Hopefully, they will have recovered all of that money by the time you reach your life expectancy. (Not all people comply with the actuaries, by the way!)

If your service ended after September 30, 1990, and you have not made a redeposit, under CSRS you still get to count the time for your eligibility; but you get NO credit for the calculation of your annuity. So your benefit isn't reduced; it simply doesn't count at all.

Under FERS, if your contributions were refunded and you do not make the redeposit, it does not count for either eligibility purposes or annuity purposes, and so in most cases it will make sense to make that redeposit under FERS. This redeposit did not used to be allowed; it was only legislation that passed in 2009, which allowed FERS employees to begin counting their sick leave in the calculation of their pension, that provided that FERS employees could make a redeposit of funds that they had previously withdrawn.

Should you make that redeposit? For CSRS, if the service was prior to October 1, 1990, we know that it's going be over 20 years of interest that gets added to the original amount that was refunded. The interest is typically more than the original refund, sometimes much more; often more than the employee can afford to take out of a lump sum and put back into that redeposit. It often makes sense just not to pay it back and take the reduction to your pension.

For FERS, because that contribution level is smaller, what you would have withdrawn was a lower amount and the timeframe is shorter. It may still make sense to make that redeposit. You're going to want to calculate it and determine whether it makes sense or not.

COUNTING MILITARY TIME

If you've served in the military, another way to change the value of your pension is to buy back for that military service to add to your creditable time. The DD214 provides a record of your military service. For CSRS employees who were employed under CSRS before October 1, 1982, you would be required to make a deposit of 7% of your basic pay while you were in the military plus interest in order to count all that time. However, there's a little loophole here for you. Even if you do not make the deposit, as long as you are not eligible for Social Security, at age 62, you get to count your military time anyway. In other words, you get a freebie! You don't have to pay back for it, and it counts toward your creditable service. On the other hand, if you should become eligible for Social Security at age 62 and you have not paid that military deposit back, at age 62, the time for that military service will be deducted from your annuity, and your annuity will be recalculated without those years of service because of your Social Security eligibility. This provision is known as Catch-62, and you want to make sure you don't get caught in it. If there is any doubt about your Social Security eligibility and you want to be absolutely certain that your military time is going to count, you're going to want to make that 7% of basic pay deposit plus interest.

If you became an employee under CSRS on or after October 1, 1982, you must make that deposit if you want the time to count. Under FERS, the deposit required for military service is less; you must make a deposit of 3% of your basic pay plus interest. If you don't make the deposit, you don't get to count the time. In almost all cases, it will make sense to pay back for your military time under FERS. It's going to add to your years of service, it may make you eligible to retire sooner, and it will increase the value of your annuity.

PART-TIME SERVICE

Part-time service can be confusing for federal employees as they get closer to retirement. For both systems – CSRS and FERS – it works the same. Any part-time service prior to April 7, 1986 counts 100% toward both eligibility and the calculation of your annuity. It all counts. Any part-time service after April 7, 1986, counts 100% towards eligibility as if you'd been working the entire time, but it is prorated for your annuity calculation. There's a very complicated formula that is used to determine what percentage of time you were actually working compared to the actual number of hours you could have been working – 2080, for example, in a year. That percentage is applied to your annuity after it has been calculated.

There's an easier way to do this if you're trying to just calculate it in your head: If you worked part-time for 10 years and you worked 32 hours per pay week, that would be the equivalent of 80% of what you could have been working, and you could take 80% of that 10 years, which would give you 8 years. Let's say your total years of service was 30 years. Rather than calculating your annuity on 30 years, it would be calculated on 28, because of the reduction for the period that you worked part-time.

That's the simple way to get an estimate; there's a much more complex formula that OPM uses to calculate your benefit. You're just trying to determine if you're in the ballpark when you're calculating these benefits yourself, so that you know what to expect.

Your Federal Employee Group Life Insurance premiums are also affected by part-time service, because the value of FEGLI is based on your actual salary. For retirement purposes, FEGLI is based on the actual salary on your last day of employment.

Part-time employees also pay more for their FEHB (or their Federal Employee Health Benefits). They pay a larger percent of the premium. The government's share is determined by dividing the number of hours you were scheduled to work during the pay period, and dividing that by the number of hours worked by a full-time employee in the same position. That percentage is applied to the government's contribution of 72% made for full-time employees, so the part-time employee ends up paying a larger percentage of their health care premiums. However, the good news is that they still have access to the health benefits. In retirement, all retirees get the same government contribution towards their FEHB premium regardless of whether or not they retired as part-time workers.

SECTION

2

THE THRIFT SAVINGS PLAN

AN INTRODUCTION

---- ★ ----

Making Money- A young man asked an old rich man how he made his money. The old guy fingered his worsted wool vest and said, "Well, son, it was 1932, the depths of the Great Depression. I was down to my last nickel.

I invested that nickel in an apple. I spent the entire day polishing the apple and, at the end of the day, i sold the apple for ten cents. The next morning, I invested those ten cents in two apples. I spent the entire day polishing them and sold them at 5:00 pm for 20 cents. I continued this system for a month, by the end of which I'd accumulated a fortune of $1.37. Then my wife's father died and left us two million dollars."

You probably do not want to rely on this method to accumulate your retirement savings, therefore please take the Chapters on TSP very seriously!

How much should I be contributing?
Where should the funds be allocated?
What do I do with my TSP when I retire?

There is no one magic formula for everyone. When you get past the emotional constraints of the TSP, it's a savings plan (notice the name – Thrift Savings Plan – not Thrift Investing Plan). You're torn between wanting to protect your hard-saved funds and earning a decent return. Understanding the difference between saving and investing can help align the expectations for your TSP.

After two major downturns with another possibly looming on the horizon, TSP participants are necessarily queasy. Understanding your options within the plan and creating a strategy that fits your retirement plan can help ease your fears and put you in control of your future.

★ ★

TIPS FOR CONTRIBUTING TO YOUR TSP

An important Thrift Savings Plan tip for a FERS participant is not to contribute too much, too soon, every year. Let's say that your goal is to contribute $17,000 - the full contribution - in one year. Some people like to increase their contributions early in the year, so that by the end of September they'll have made the full contribution of $17,000. They look forward to some extra take-home pay for the holidays. But if you do this, you're going miss out on your agency's matching contributions. If you're contributing at least 5%, you're going to get a 5% match, spread out evenly over all 26 pay periods. If your intent is to contribute the maximum, which in the year 2012 is $17,000, be sure it's distributed equally over 26 periods.

It doesn't mean that you have to contribute the same amount all year; you can change your contribution level throughout the year. You just want to determine that you're consistently contributing at least 5%. Otherwise, you're giving up a valuable contribution from the government.

★ ★

CHAPTER 4

YOUR TSP; A VALUABLE TOOL

I f you are an employee under the FERS System, TSP is designed to be 1/3 of your income in retirement, although it can represent anywhere from 30 to 50 percent depending on your career longevity. It's crucial not only that you maximize your savings, but that you also know how to manage your portfolio by making prudent investment decisions based on what's right for you. In the Thrift Savings Plan, the conflict is that it is a thrift savings plan, not an investing plan, and yet you're asked to think like investors.

You're told to be in the market by using the C, S and I Funds. The conflict comes when people recognize, "Well, I'm saving my money – and now I have to invest it, too." It really is a savings plan, not an investment plan, so keep the savings piece at the forefront. Obviously, you want the best returns you can get and you want to have a working knowledge and understanding of your options. If you keep in mind that it is a savings plan as opposed to an investment plan, it will help you as you go about making those choices.

Let's begin by looking at a short history of the Thrift Savings Plan and how we got where we are today. In this chapter, we'll also look at what the future holds for TSP, some magic numbers associated with TSP, and borrowing from your TSP. The two most critical points are allocating your Thrift Savings Plan and the challenges posed by the volatile market. You'll also have the opportunity to hear from a colleague who's the leading analyst at MyTSPVision, a web-based research service for TSP participants. He'll share some ideas for allocating your TSP that you may not have considered before. Finally, we'll look at the most common question I hear from federal employees at retirement, "How can I create income from my TSP?"

A SHORT HISTORY OF THE TSP

The Thrift Savings Plan was implemented in April 1987 with one fund - the G Fund. Two additional funds were added in January of 1988 - the F Fund and the C Fund. These three funds remained the foundation of the TSP until the S and I funds were added in 2001.

For those of you who participated in the TSP from the early days, you'll recall that there were percentage limits on how much of your salary you could contribute. Initially, FERS participants were allowed to contribute 5% and CSRS weren't allowed to participate at all. Once CSRS was finally allowed to contribute, their limits were always 5% less than the FERS limits. When FERS could contribute 10%, CSRS could only contribute 5%. In 2006, the contribution limits changed, allowing all employees to contribute up to the IRS-established limit, making it very similar to private 401K plans.

The total amount in the plan fluctuates (sometimes wildly), but for most of 2011 there was roughly $300 billion in the Thrift Savings Plan, with about 4.5 million participants. This makes it the largest defined contribution plan in the United States. For the first 12 years of the TSP's existence, the stock market, and thus the TSP's only equity offering, the C Fund, went straight up. During that time, the average annual return for the C Fund was 19.41%. What a great way to save for retirement!

Federal employees were lulled into complacency believing they were brilliant investors who didn't have to think about how to allocate their savings. They just had to make sure they were doing a good job saving and putting that money into the fund. When asked now about how they make their TSP investment decisions, I hear things like, "I just leave it where it was when I started working," or, "Bob in our office is really a good investor, so I just make my decisions based on what he tells me to do." Reminder - an investment strategy that's appropriate for one individual might be completely inappropriate for another; it needs to be a personal decision.

Many participants also confess to a "don't ask – don't tell" strategy. "I don't open my envelope when I get my statement because I don't want to look at it. If I don't look at it, everything's okay." They've chosen to live in a bubble, hoping that what they don't know won't hurt them.

Younger TSP participants tend to think, "I'm young. I'm going to take all the risk that I can get. The rules of Wall Street say that if I am willing to take on more risk, I will be rewarded with higher returns," which isn't always the case. In fact, if you look at the average return in the C Fund, which mirrors the S&P 500 Index, over the past 10 years, from 2001 through 2010, the average annual return was 1.4 percent.[1] When you're planning for retirement, 1.4 percent is not enough to cover things like inflation and taxes.

THE TSP FUNDS

Let's look at the five individual funds in this Thrift Savings Plan, starting with the safest fund and progressing to the riskiest.

The G and the F Funds are the TSP's fixed income funds. The G Fund is the government securities investment fund and it invests in short-term U.S. Treasuries that are specially issued to the TSP. So, unless you're a TSP participant, you're not able to invest in the G Fund. The G Fund is the safest of the TSP funds because there's no risk of loss. The G fund offers you the opportunity to earn rates of interest similar to those of long-term government securities. But again, what's really being issued is short-term U.S. Treasury securities with no risk of loss of principal because payment of principal and interest is guaranteed by the U.S. Government. Of course, there's risk that the economy will experience inflation, and that your fund's value won't keep up with buying power. But when you're looking purely for safety, the G Fund is the safest fund out of the five TSP funds.

The returns of the remaining four funds are tied to different indexes, but they do have a number of characteristics in common. All of them are passively managed index funds, and the current fund manager is Black Rock Institutional Trust Company.

The F Fund is a fixed income index investment fund; a bond fund that tracks the Barclay's Capital U.S. Aggregate Fund Index, which was formerly Lehman Brothers U.S. Aggregate Bond Index.

It's a broad index, representing government, mortgaged-backed corporate and non-corporate, and foreign government sectors of the bond market. It's comprised of high-quality, fixed income securities with maturities of more than one year. The F Fund offers you the opportunity to earn rates of return that may exceed money market funds over the long term, particularly during periods of declining interest rates like those that we've experienced over the past 10 years. The F Fund has been one of the highest performers of all the TSP funds over the past 10 years with low risk. The main risk in the F Fund consists of nonpayment of interest or principal, or credit risk, which is relatively low because it only includes investment-grade securities, which are broadly diversified. Another risk for the F Fund is prepayment risk; the risk that the security will be repaid before it matures, causing loss to investors of additional interest. Lastly, there is risk to those investing in the F Fund should interest rates rise, because in a rising interest rate environment the prices of bonds typically fall.

The C, S, and I are TSP's equity funds. While they're the riskiest funds, they also have the potential for higher returns. The C Fund, or Common Stock Investment Fund, is the second most participated-in fund among TSP participants, behind the G Fund. The objective of the C Fund is to replicate the S&P 500 Index, which is made up of stocks of 500 large- to medium-sized U.S. companies that are traded in the U.S. Stock Market. This index represents 10 major industry groups, and the stocks in it represent about 75% of the market value of the United States Stock Market. The C Fund offers you the potential to earn high investment returns over the long term, from a broadly diversified selection of stocks. The earnings in the C Fund consist of gains or losses of these stocks, and also any dividend income that these stocks are paying.

The S Fund is the Small Capitalization Stock Investment Fund. It tracks the Dow Jones total stock market index, which contains all the common stocks (except those in the S&P 500, which are in the C Fund) that are actively traded in the U.S. Stock Market. Like the C Fund, earnings in the S Fund consist of either gains or losses of stocks along with dividend income.

The last of the five TSP funds is the I Fund, which is the International Stock Index Investment Fund. The I Fund tracks the Morgan Stanley Capital International EAFE (Europe, Australasia and Far East) Index. This index is invested primarily in large companies in 21 developed countries, not in emerging countries.

In deciding where to invest your money in the TSP, you should consider not only returns, but also potential risk. There has to be balance. Of course, everyone wants the highest return possible – but are you clear on the level of risk? Do you understand what the maximum loss is that you can handle before you're forced to run for your bottle of Advil or whiskey, or a package of Depends? It's critical to diversify your accounts in an allocation that is appropriate for you, with an eye to your retirement time horizon.

In 2005, the TSP introduced their Lifecycle Funds, or L Funds, specifically for participants who wanted the convenience of having their investments managed for them. The best thing about these L Funds is that you only need to answer one question: When will you need the money in your TSP account after you leave federal service? Once you determine what that anticipated date is, you'll pick the Lifecycle Fund with the nearest date to your target retirement date. When the Lifecycle Fund was introduced, TSP said that you can be assured that your allocation is professionally designed, low cost, and virtually maintenance-free. All of the Lifecycle Funds are comprised of those five underlying funds within TSP. Currently, the riskiest

Lifecycle Fund is the L2050, which is designed for somebody whose retirement date is anywhere from 2045 and beyond. Every quarter, the funds are rebalanced, so that they're continually getting more conservative as you get closer to retirement. When you get to your retirement date they will go to the most conservative L fund, 30 percent of which is in equities, and that's where your money will stay.

Now, becoming increasingly conservative with your money as you get closer to retirement, with no effort on your part, sounds like a beautiful thing. But the problem I find is that most participants don't use the lifecycle funds as they were intended to be used, which is to choose the lifecycle fund closest to the date that you are going to retire. Instead the participants spread their investments out across several Lifecycle Funds, along with the individual funds in the mistaken assumption that this makes their holdings more diverse.[2] The reality is they don't have any idea what their actual holdings are or, more importantly, how much risk they are subjecting their portfolio to.

★ ★

When I'm meeting with a client and we're looking at their TSP funds, I'll say, "How do you have your TSP funds invested?" And a typical response will be, "Oh, I have 20% in the G Fund and 10 percent in the F Fund and I have a little bit in the C and S, and I have those Lifecycle Funds too. I have the 2030 Fund and I have the 2020 fund and I'm really diversified." When I ask them what is the total percentage that they have in each of the funds, or what the overall percentage is of equity holdings and bond holdings, most TSP participants that invest this way have no clue. The really bad news is they also don't have any idea how much risk they are taking with their retirement funds.

★ ★

The other problem we've found is that when we're going through rocky, turbulent times in the market, changes in investment strategy need to be considered. Unfortunately, the only change the Lifecycle Fund makes is to get more conservative and shift more into bonds as people get close to their retirement. They do not react to what's going on in the economy or in the Stock Market. In turbulent markets like those we experienced in the first decade of this century, Lifecycle Funds really took a hit. This was particularly hard for those who were close to retirement and had thought that they were safe in Lifecycle Funds, when they suffered losses of 10% or more.

WHAT'S AHEAD FOR THE
THRIFT SAVINGS PLAN?

What does the future hold for Thrift Savings Plans? In 2009, the TSP board added four provisions that became legislation. The first was the creation of a Roth TSP. Most participants were excited about that, because in times of low tax-rate environments like those we're experiencing now, they'd be able to contribute to their Thrift Savings Plan after tax and have that grow tax deferred, just as in a regular Roth IRA. The benefit is that earnings will be income tax-free when withdrawn. Unfortunately, at this writing, in late 2011, that plan still has not been implemented. The TSP Board has said that the Roth TSP is expected to be available mid 2012.

A recent innovation, begun in August 2010, was automatic enrollment in the TSP for new federal employees. This was a wonderful idea; as a young person, the last thing you're likely to be thinking about is saving for retirement, so this ensures that 3% of your paycheck is put into in the Thrift Savings Plan. Employees can choose to opt out; if not, their money is automatically invested into the lower-risk G Fund, although they can choose higher-risk funds if they wish.

Another addition is new survivorship options. Prior to 2009, if a participant in TSP passed away, the surviving spouse had to take their money out of the Thrift Saving Plan. Under this new legislation, the spouse can choose to leave the funds in TSP, while rolling it over into their own IRA.

One of the last of the provisions in the 2009 legislation was the option to create mutual fund choices, which were investments in TSP. In weighing the pros and cons of that choice, the negatives seem to outweigh the positives. First, by adding more mutual fund investment options, you're also adding responsibility for the TSP Board to provide information about those funds. Frankly, many TSP participants feel that the existing five funds are confusing enough, especially when you add the Lifecycle Funds.

Another downside to creating more mutual fund choices is the cost involved. The TSP Board members pride themselves on their ability to offer very low-cost investment options. The cost in TSP funds is .025 percent – for every $1,000 invested, your expense is about 25 cents. This is unheard of in the private sector, where the average cost for a 401(k) is supposed to be from .70 to 1.4. Now that the Department of Labor is drilling down on the transparency of 401(k)'s, they're finding that the fees are often actually much higher than that, up to 2% to 3%.

MAGIC NUMBERS

In 2012, the contribution limits for this Thrift Savings Plan are $17,000, if you're under age 50. If you're age 50 or older, you can contribute an additional $5,500. CSRS and CSRS offset employees don't get a match. However, if you're under the FERS Retirement System or a FERS transferee, as long as you're contributing 5%, you'll get a match of 5%. Even if a FERS employee isn't contributing anything, his agency will give him an automatic 1% match. That's a pretty good deal; very rarely do I see federal employees that are not contributing at least 5%. And if they're not, I lock them in my office until they make the phone call and contribute the full five, because there's certainly nothing better than free money.

At age 55, you can have access to your Thrift Savings Plan without a 10% excise penalty if you separate service or retire at age

55 or later. That's important, because sometimes people think "Well, if I retire at 54, I'll leave my money in TSP and then when I turn 55 I'll have access to it without the early withdrawal penalty" – but that's absolutely not true. They must retire at age 55 or later to have access to that money without a 10% penalty.

At age 59½, TSP participants can access their TSP for a one-time, penalty-free withdrawal if they're still working. A lot of federal employees have done that in order to convert some of their TSP into a Roth IRA. Another reason you may want to make that one-time withdrawal is if you have another investment that is performing better for you than TSP. If you do choose to make that one-time withdrawal, you can't take anything else out of TSP until retirement. If you retire at age 59½, you have access to your TSP without a 10% early withdrawal penalty.

The next of the "magic numbers" is 70½. If you're retired and your money's still with TSP, when you turn 70½ you must begin taking your minimum distributions from your TSP and other tax-qualified accounts. If you're still working, you don't have to take those required minimum distributions.

The last magic number is $1 million. Those of you who read financial publications like Kiplinger's or Money magazine are probably convinced that, in order to have a successful retirement, you need to get $1 million into your TSP portfolio. While that may or may not be true for individuals outside of the federal government, remember that if you're under the CSRS system, the majority of your retirement is going to come from your pension. Thus, you're not going to know what that magic number for your account value should really be unless you do some planning on your own, or work with the expertise of a financial advisor. Even for the FERS retirement system, you might not need as much as you would if you were invested in an outside 401K, because you still have that FERS pension component as part of your overall retirement.

The only way to know your magic number is by planning. In order to plan wisely, you first have to give serious thought to what you want your retirement lifestyle to be, and what it will cost. How much income will you need in retirement? There are calculators you can use to figure that number or you can work with an advisor to come up with that figure. Once you know your goal, you need to determine if you are on the right track towards meeting that goal. If not, now is the time to make the changes necessary to get you there.

TSP LOAN PROGRAMS

Another program offered to you while you're still working is TSP loans. There are two types of loans. The first is a general loan that gives you up to five years to repay. There's no documentation involved; you just let them know that you need a loan and they'll provide you with it. The maximum that you can borrow is either $50,000, or 50% of your current invested balance. Even if your invested balance is $500,000, the maximum that you could borrow is $50,000. That also applies to a residential loan. The difference is that, with a residential loan, you can take 15 years to repay. It does require documentation; you have to show them that you're using the loan to purchase a home. You can apply on paper, using TSP20 Loan Application or you can apply online. The only cost involved is the $50 application fee, and the interest rate as of this writing is 2.5%.

It's a pretty nice option to have, but there are risks. When you're making this loan repayment, you may contribute less to your Thrift Savings Plan, because you only have so much in your paycheck.

The other risk is that, if your TSP earns a higher return then that loan interest rate, you're going have less in TSP. If the interest rate is 2½%, you've effectively got an interest-free loan. You're paying yourself back, because you're generating that 2½%. But if your money could have been earning 8% or 9% in some other investment, you're missing out on that opportunity. You should know, too, that residential loans are not considered mortgages, so your interest is not deductible on your tax return. The other thing to consider is that your loan is being paid with after-tax dollars. You're putting pre-tax dollars into your TSP, then you're borrowing it – but that money you're paying back is being paid with after-tax dollars.

REALLOCATING YOUR TSP

The last thing I want touch on is reallocating your TSP. A few years back, the Thrift Savings Board limited the amount of times you could do inter-fund transfers, and now you're only allowed to do two inter-fund transfers per month. The only exception to the rule is the G Fund, to which you can transfer funds as often as you wish, with no restrictions. But I was at a workshop recently where someone from TSP told me that 97% of participants never move money in a year – they just leave it on cruise control. So let's talk about what's really important in allocating your TSP, and how you should invest it. How much risk do you hold in your portfolio, and are you comfortable with that risk?

A few years back, I was at a conference with a lot of other investment advisors, including a gentleman named Brad Kasper. Brad's firm, LSA Analytics, provides analytics and research on a variety of investments to financial advisors and 401K providers. I use their analytics for my private clients and have found it a tremendous benefit to my practice. Unfortunately, they were not doing analytics on TSP. I asked Brad if they could look into adding TSP to their research platform. The problem was they didn't have the tools they needed to go inside TSP, get the data and put it together in a meaningful strategy.

About a year after that, I got a call from LSA. They'd informed me that they found a way to look at TSP funds as part of their proprietary system, and put meaningful portfolios together. Up until that point, TSP participants could go to the TSP website, and get information on the TSP Funds. What the website didn't say, because they had no way of predicting it, was how much risk was out there. Historically it has averaged 10%, 15%, 20%. But how much risk do you hold in your portfolio, and are you comfortable with that risk?

I would like to turn this part over to Brad Kasper, who is the leading analyst at MyTSPVision.com, a website created to assist federal employees with allocating their Thrift Savings Plan in a strategy that is appropriate for them. It also provides subscribers with continuous updates on changes in the economy and markets that might warrant making changes to their TSP. This is not a "buy and hold" strategy. Nor is it a trading strategy where you're trading the market on a daily, weekly, or monthly basis. But it's a way to manage these passively indexed funds into a more meaningful strategy for TSP participants. Now, here's Brad …

In my role as an analyst in a research firm, we found it troublesome that, with these millions of federal employees accessing the TSP plan, they don't have access to what we defined as sufficient data. How do you accurately define how much risk is associated with each one of the investments that are available to you?

For us, the challenge was, can we bring these into our systems? Can we come up with a way to track the funds and provide powerful reporting that's available to federal employees? So we started uploading some of the monthly feeds that are available through the TSP website. We were able to start generating these inside our systems and give a level look into what these funds are actually comprised of.

Today, we not only do the reporting on the funds that are available, we also provide recommended allocation strategies, because there are a lot of federal employees out there who are not getting sufficient information on how to allocate their portfolios inside the TSP plan, and are unsure about their choices. What we wanted to do was help them to understand what's available to them, with ideas of how to build a meaningful portfolio for their retirement.

There are some common problems that the average investor runs into, problems they encounter because they adhere to outdated concepts of investing. When I'm giving my presentation to investors, called "What Wall Street Told Us To Do," there are two questions that I always ask the group. The first is, "How many people in this group have heard of these two concepts? Concept number one: Be a long-term investor." Usually, everyone in the room raises his hand. "Concept number two: If you're willing to take higher risk, over time you'll be rewarded with higher returns." Again, most hands go up.

What I'd like to do is to debunk these myths. The notion of being a long-term investor comes from the "buy and hold" strategy, one that worked extremely well back in the '80s and '90s. But the reason it worked so well is that we had a booming economy and a booming market, with close to 1,000% returns on the Dow Jones Industrial Average over that time frame. You could go out and pick an investment, hold onto it, and you'd do just fine. A lot of federal employees who began their investing in the late '80s and '90s became accustomed to the notion of buying and holding as a guarantee of great returns. Many of them did very well. But for that concept to work, you have to have two things. First of all, you have to have time for that average return to work, and you have to have guts to stomach all the market volatilities you're going to encounter, in order to get the returns that the markets are generating.

There's a report out there that a lot of financial sales people use, utilizing a chart that shows what happens to an index over a long period of time. (Notice, please, that I'm going to differentiate financial sales people from financial advisors. Sales people always have something that's product-driven, something they're selling. Financial advisors educate their clients, and are not salespeople.)

The example that we use in our presentation is the S&P 500, which is probably the most broad-based index that's available. For federal employees who don't understand what the S&P 500 is, it's made up of the same stocks that make up the C Fund inside their TSP plan. If you're looking at performance of the S&P 500 over a 15-year time frame, you'll see that the average return in the S&P 500 was 8.18%. That's a pretty decent return over a 15-year time frame, one that everyone should be comfortable with. But a financial salesperson will use that data to support the "buy and hold" strategy by showing you what happens to your annual return over those 15 years if you missed the best 10 days, or the best 20, 30, or 40 days. If you missed the best 10 days, your average return dropped down to 4.83%; if you missed the best 20 days, it dropped down to 2.62%; if you missed the best 30 days, it dropped 0.02%. And if you missed the best 40 days over that 15 year time frame, your average return dropped to -1.87%.

Now, these are fascinating numbers - but they're built around what these financial salespeople are trying to get you to do. They're trying to get you to stay invested, to buy and hold, because typically they're selling you a product, and when you move your money away from a product, they're going be losing revenues.

If "buy and hold" is a concept that worked in the '80s and '90s, would it also hold true of a longer-term time frame in the overall market? To answer that question, we took a snapshot of the Dow Jones Industrial Average over 115 years, and broke that 115-year period into two different types of market cycles; bear markets, which is where markets are going down, and bull markets, when markets are doing well. Over that 115-year time frame, there were four bear markets and four bull markets. The Dow's first bull market was nine years long, and it was a 148% move on the Dow. The second time frame was five years in the '20s, right before the Depression. Over those five years, the Dow Jones was up 294%. If we were to fast-forward into the mid-'50s, we had an 11-year time frame of 154% return on the Dow. Fast-forwarding again, to the '80s and '90s, we saw 17 years of bull market returns, 1,003% on the Dow Jones Industrial Average. So we have 9 years, 5 years, 11 years and 17 years. And my question is, which of these is the one that stands out?

Over 115 years, the '80s and '90s were the anomaly of bull markets, a period in our history where we had sound economic growth and markets were just screaming up. You could probably have thrown a dart at the wall in the '80s and '90s and made 20% off of it. But this wasn't the typical bull market. In fact, it was almost double what you see in the average bull market over that 115-year time frame.

But let's take a look at the other side of that coin. What about the bear markets, when markets are going down? The first bear market lasted 18 years, with a -4.29% return on the Dow Jones Industrial Average, 18 years in which you had negative growth in overall markets. Let's fast-forward to the next one, going into the Depression right before the '30s. In that 25-year time frame, the Dow Jones grew 1.69%. If we fast-forward to the next bear market, we get into the '70s. You had 17 years of a bear market with 0.83%. And if we fast-forward beyond that all the way up to 2011, as of today, we are actually flat for the last 13 years; we're 13 years into the current bear market.

The big question is, where do we go from here? One conclusion we could reasonably draw from looking at this 115-year history of the Dow is that the average bear market is about 19 years long. But, of the bull markets that we've experienced over this 115 years, the '80s and '90s are the anomaly over that time frame. This is the period in which most federal employees started investing, and in which Wall Street successfully promoted this notion of buy and hold; don't leave, just hang with it and you're going to be okay.

We believe that that advice is a disservice to today's investor, because it's based on a concept that was created in response to these anomaly years in the '80s and '90s. What we've experienced over the last 13 years is more traditional, with a lot of up-, down-, and sideways-moving markets. Yes, there's a general trend upward – but overall, we are in a more typical market environment today than we were in the '80s and '90s. Financial salespeople promote the idea that you're going to be penalized if you move your money away. And we saw what happens when you missed the best days – but why doesn't anyone ask what happens if you were to miss the worst days in the markets?

As it happens, somebody did. BTN Research did a 25-year study on the S&P 500. Average annual return over that period was 9.8%. What would have happened if we were to miss the 25 worst days over that 25-year time frame? As it turns out, if you'd missed the worst 25 days over that 25-year time frame, your average return would have jumped 17.8%, a little different side of the story here. Financial salespeople don't generally share this side of the story because it doesn't necessarily support their "buy and hold" strategy.

We think this "buy and hold"/"be a long term investor" stuff is effectively a self-serving message generated by Wall Street and utilized on Main Street. It's a concept that was so ingrained in the '80s and '90s that it's very difficult to teach people to think otherwise. When we meet with federal employees, we still see these big weightings inside the C Fund, because this is what they've been taught to do. But the data above should help you adjust your thinking.

Onto the second myth – that if you're willing to take high risk over a period of time, you'll be rewarded with higher returns. Traditionally stocks have more risk associated with them than bonds, so the implication here is that if I'm willing to take more risk inside stocks versus bonds, I'm going be rewarded with higher returns over time.

Let's compare stocks versus bonds, using the S&P 500 and the Barclay's Capital U.S. Bond Aggregate. For you federal employees, we're comparing the C Fund to the F Fund. When we look at the C Fund versus the F Fund over the last one-, three-, five-, and ten-year basis, on a ten-year basis, the C Fund had a -0.75% return. The F Fund, which is the bond fund, earned 7.10%. This shows bonds out-performing stocks by a little over 7% over the last ten years - the first time in history that bonds have consecutively outperformed equities or stocks in this time frame. Bonds are clearly an asset class that has less than a third of the risk represented by stocks. So – you have the F Fund, taking less than a third of the risk of the C Fund, just shy of 8% of annual average outperformance over the last ten years. Where was the benefit for taking additional risks inside stocks in that period?

Am I telling you to put all your money into bonds? Absolutely not. The point of this is to help you to understand different investments that are available to you. This is why it's so important to understand the risk characteristics associated with the funds. For too long, federal employees have had to live off the research of a two-page snapshot that provides a quick composite of the funds that are available inside the TSP, without access to information on what the associated risks were with the specific funds available to them. Looking at these numbers made us realize that we have to be able to provide better research.

That said, the Thrift Savings Plan has made huge strides. Their new website and some of the tools that they have now are a lot better than they were even two years ago. But it's our goal to make this understanding intuitive to you, so that we stop thinking about investing the way Wall Street told us to think for so many years, and address how we start building meaningful portfolios.

Once we have research on the funds available to us, we still have the problem of how we diversify it. How do we allocate our portfolio? Most people understand diversification to mean "don't put all your eggs in one basket." Here's a better definition of diversification: It's a risk management technique that fixes a wide variety of investments within a portfolio. The rationale behind this technique contends that a portfolio of different kinds of investments will, on average, yield higher returns and pose lower risk than an individual investment found within the portfolio. So again, what those who promote diversification are saying is, spread your eggs amongst many baskets. And that makes sense to a lot of people.

But there's a second part to this definition that most investors don't know, and it's that the benefits of diversification will hold only if the securities in the portfolio are not perfectly correlated. Typically, when I say correlated, the investor is looking at me as if I'm speaking another language, so let's define "correlation." I'll give you a practical example: I have an older brother and younger brother. My older brother was the leader. Whatever he did, my younger brother and I would always follow suit. This was wonderful if he was helping Mom carry in the groceries, because then we were all helping Mom carry in the groceries.

But what if he was doing something bad? What happened if he got into Mom's 'fridge and started drinking a beer, and so the rest of us started drinking beer, too? All of a sudden, we're all doing something bad. I would define us as highly correlated kids. The problem with correlation in that situation is that it's great when things are going well, when he's doing good things. But when he's being bad, all of a sudden it's an absolute nightmare.

For an investment example, let's look at 2008 and performance numbers. A lot of people used to think, "Okay, if I have my large-cap stock funds and my small-cap stock funds, my C Fund, my S Fund, I also need to diversify and be inside International. So I go and get invested in the I Fund." You might have thought that you were well diversified with those three positions in 2008 – until you saw the C Fund lose 37%, the S Fund drop 38.32%, and the I Fund drop 42.43%.

So, you tell me – where was the protection out of those three funds? You might argue that you'd spread your eggs out, and that you were diversified. But if you were in a highly correlated position, then you did not have a well-diversified portfolio. In fact, the only way to find protection back in 2008 was to go beyond and find that protection inside the G Fund, which was up 3.73%, or have the insight to have positions inside the S Fund, which was up 5.46%. But how often are the F Fund and G Fund talked about in terms of an overall investment strategy? Most people look at the G Fund as an absolutely boring fund. It does the same darn thing every month.

These days it's looking like a pretty exciting fund, because people want that consistency and performance. The F Fund has never been an overly attractive fund. Back in the '80s and '90s, you saw equity outperform that F Fund, hands down. Investors ignored them, didn't incorporate these funds Into their portfolios, and thus were not truly balanced or diversified.

That's where we come in. We try to build portfolios with this balanced approach, around a concept that we call winning by not losing, which means finding protection when markets are going down. We do not adhere to the "buy and hold" strategy, because too often "buy and hold" actually means "stomach the worst and over a longer period of time, you'll be able to get average returns."

But most investors don't want to be average, and they certainly don't want to stomach the worst. In fact, typically when investors have to stomach the worst, what do they do? They capitulate and hit the sidelines. Then when these markets turn around, they don't have any money invested in them. They just suffered the worst part of the downturn, and the money's sitting in cash or in a protective position. When the markets turn back around, they're still at low values inside their accounts. It's a very simple concept; we all want to buy low and sell high. But it's almost impossible to adhere to that, because our emotions prompt us to do the complete opposite. When markets are down we're fearful, and we do not want to buy in. When markets are high, we're happy; we're comfortable, we want to buy in.

That is the trap that most investors fall into and that's the trap that My TSP Vision portfolios are trying to get federal employees out of. And it's by utilizing the research; it's by building what we consider to be more diversified port-folios that, again, are built around the concept of winning by not losing over a longer period of time, protecting first and promoting growth second.

CREATING INCOME FROM TSP

Everything that we've been talking about prior to this is about saving and allocating your TSP. But what happens at retirement? You've put in 30 years working for the federal government. You've done a good job making contributions, and managing your TSP. Now that you're ready to retire, how do you turn that investment into a monthly check?

To understand the difference between accumulation and distri-bution from the Thrift Savings Plan, I like to use the analogy of the difference between climbing Mount Everest and descending from it. There are strategies that you'll need to employ when you're making that ascent to the summit – and very different strategies to use coming down the mountain.

As an example, let's go back and look at the S&P 500, which is your C Fund. Looking at the period from September 2000 through September 2002, if you were invested in the C Fund, your account would have dropped by 44.73%. If you were able to stomach that fall and stayed in the C Fund, you would have recovered by October 2006. So if you'd had a $100,000 investment, it would have gone down to $55,270, but as long as you had the guts to stick it out, you would have recovered.

Now, let's look at that same market shift if you'd been retired and taking income. Again, in this example you have $100,000 in your Thrift Savings Plan. It's all in the C Fund and you're paying yourself a check in the amount of $500 per month – then comes the downturn. If you were in the C Fund taking monthly distributions from September 2000 through September 2002, you would have dropped by 44.73 percent, if you're looking at the performance reports of the S&P 500. However, because you're taking that distribution, your account value would actually have dropped down to $42,770. In reality, if that happened, the average person is not going to stick it out. They're going to shut it down and get out of the C Fund, and lock in their losses. That's what many federal employees did during that period, because what was required to get back up to that $100,000 would be a return of 133 percent and that wasn't possible during that term.

So, how can we design a plan for taking income to assure that you're not going to outlive your money? In creating income from your TSP in retirement, there are really two chances to take distributions at retirement. You can either do a partial withdrawal, using form TSP-77, or a full withdrawal, using form TSP-70.

Let's talk about those two before we look at the other options. If you're going to take a partial withdrawal, you only have the opportunity to do that one time. If you want to take another withdrawal after that, TSP is going to make you take everything out. The other option for leaving your money in TSP and taking a full withdrawal is using that TSP-70 form, where you're going use that form but you can actually take monthly withdrawals. Many TSP participants choose that option.

You do need to be cautious, however, and here's why: Let's say you decided to take $800 a month out of TSP, but you realize by June that's really more than you need to cover your expenses. So you call TSP and say, "Can you stop withdrawing from my account until the end the year?" Be prepared to hear something like this, "No, however we can change the amount of your monthly withdrawals, but not until January."

Let's also consider this scenario: You're taking $800 a month, supplementing your income, and you have an emergency. Maybe your car breaks down or you need a new roof – whatever the reason, you suddenly need to take a lump sum out of your TSP. Now you call TSP, explain that you're taking your monthly withdrawal and ask if you can take $10,000 out of your account – and again, they're going tell you "no." You didn't elect that, and if you want to make that withdrawal, you're going to have to take it all out.

Many retirees leave their money in TSP because of the big advantage of having low-cost index funds. Just be aware that, even though it is your money, you don't have the full flexibility that you may have with some other choices. I'm not here to tell you to roll it over into an IRA, although that's certainly a choice, because you have more options. If you feel that there is a better investment option for you outside of TSP, it may make a lot of sense for you to roll it over into an IRA, because you'll have more control of it.

The other way to create income from your Thrift Savings Plan is through an immediate annuity. When you do that, you're turning it over to MetLife Insurance Company. There are a lot of choices – whether you want to take single life or joint life payout, whether you want to have cost of living – but once you make that decision, it's irrevocable.

Let's look at an example. Say you had $200,000 in your Thrift Savings Plan, you were single, and you wanted the maximum payout to you. (Most people don't do this; more often, they'd elect to have at least a cash refund if they passed away before the funds are paid out them.) You retire, a couple months go by, you're getting your monthly check from MetLife – then you go outside, cross the street, get hit by a car and die. What happens to the balance of your lifetime savings? Well, unfortunately in that example, MetLife would keep it. So, typically I don't recommend that anyone take the annuity option because it's an irrevocable decision, and we all know that, as you go through life, there are going to be changes.

Another thing I've seen happen, although very rarely in working with federal employees, is a spendthrift mentality setting in. There are people out there that think, "Okay, now I'm retired, I have this account and I'm going to have a great time with it." Five years later, their account has run dry.

I saw this happen to a retiree named Nancy. She and I had done some income planning; she had a pension, and we were supplementing her income with her TSP. We'd created a plan for her that she felt pretty comfortable with, one which she felt would meet her income needs. A year went by and she called my office, wanting to withdraw a fairly substantial amount. That was fine, of course – it was her money – but we cautioned her that she wouldn't be able to maintain net income for life by taking such large withdrawals at the rate that she was taking it. She said she understood, but explained that her daughter was getting married and she wanted to give her a nice wedding.

Then six months go by, and she calls for another withdrawal. This time it was for her son; he was out of work and he needed help. And so it went. Within three years, her account went down to zero. You have to understand that it's not your employer giving you this monthly check anymore. You've created this bucket of assets, and now you have to be responsible for creating income and for making that last throughout your life.

Let's look at an example of creating income. What I'd like to do is discuss the annuity through MetLife. Right now, the current rate that MetLife is paying is 2.25 percent. Let's call our retiree Mary; Mary has a balance of $300,000 in her TSP. She's the TSP participant, and she and her husband Bob are both 65 years old. Mary chooses to take the annuity, but she chooses to have a joint life payout with her spouse.

If either Mary or her husband Bob should pass away, that payment's going to continue regardless, until the second spouse passes away. They've opted for level payments, which is higher than it would have been to have increasing payments for cost of living. At least it starts out a lot higher and, again, it's a 100 percent survivor annuity. If Mary passes away, Bob's still going to get the same payout and vice versa. According to the TSP calculator, the monthly payment for Mary would be $1,339, which would be paid out over her lifetime.

Now, let's consider some alternatives. As I mentioned, you can certainly roll your TSP over to an IRA and manage it yourself, but you don't want to do that unless you're sure that it makes sense, and you have some type of plan for creating income. A lot of my clients are creating income from TSP with a strategy we call sequential income planning. By utilizing sequential income planning, you're simply creating income over different time periods. It's another option for securing income from your TSP. So, assuming that Mary starts out with $300,000 in her TSP, we're going to look at creating income and a strategy we call income bucket planning.

SEQUENTIAL INCOME PLANNING

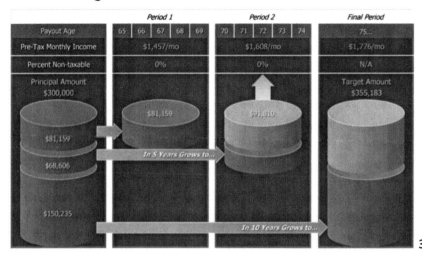

	Period 1	Period 2	Final Period
Payout Age	65 66 67 68 69	70 71 72 73 74	75...
Pre-Tax Monthly Income	$1,457/mo	$1,608/mo	$1,776/mo
Percent Non-taxable	0%	0%	N/A
Principal Amount $300,000	$81,159 / In 5 Years Grows to...	$91,810	Target Amount $355,183
	$81,159		
	$68,606		
	$150,235 / In 10 Years Grows to...		

3

What Mary does with the $300,000 from her TSP is, first, to leave $81,159 in her TSP, which we're going to put it in the G Fund because we want to make sure that it's guaranteed. She's going to take income immediately, so we want that asset to be guaranteed. At the same time, she's going to roll over the balance of her TSP to two other investment options.

For the first five years of Mary's retirement, she's going to draw income in the amount of $1,457 a month and after five years, that TSP account will be spent down. Meanwhile, when she retired, she had taken the balance and put it into two other investment accounts. One was set up with $68,606, and that went into an index annuity.[4] The index annuity allows Mary to participate in higher excess interest rates over the long term. Index annuity returns have been anywhere from 0, if there's no gain, to 15% or 16%. On average, returns for indexed annuities have been 4% to 6%. So, in this example, we assume that the $68,000 she's invested would grow by 5% and in that sixth year, when her TSP account is spent down, she's going to start taking income from this annuity. In this example, she's going to annuitize it for five years. After five years we're assuming that $68,606 will have grown to $91,810. That will pay out $1,608 each month to Mary for the next five years. If she passes away during that time, it'll pay out to whoever she's designated as her beneficiary.

At the end of that second five years, that account is also going to be drawn down. Now, her third account (or her third "bucket"), was opened with $150,230. Where you'd want to put this money depends on your risk profile, but in this case we're looking at taking a portion of income and creating a guaranteed income stream over Mary's lifetime. In this example, I used all guaranteed accounts. So this third bucket, $150,235, also went to a fixed index annuity, but we added an income rider. There are many companies that offer this, and the particular company we used was paying an 8.2% compound annual increase to create a withdrawal account, at the point in time that Mary is ready to start taking income.

Based on having this account grow by 8.2%, and roll up to $355,180 for income purposes, now she can take $1,776 a month and that's guaranteed over her lifetime, as well as Bob's.

So no matter what happens — even if her account value actually went down to zero — as long as she has that guaranteed income rider and she stays within the withdrawal limitations of the annuity, she is guaranteed that $1,776 a month. If she and Bob both pass away, anything left in her account would pass on to whomever she's named as designated beneficiaries.

If we go back and compare this to the TSP annuity, with its monthly payments of $1,551 that would stop when both she and her husband pass away, versus having anywhere from $1,457 a month up to $1,776 a month, this option allows for some flexibility.

What if Mary decides she wants additional money? She's been taking withdrawals for the first five years out of her TSP, but suddenly Mary finds that she needs more money than $1,457 a month because she wants to go and buy herself a new car. In this scenario, she has her money in her other accounts. She's not annuitized that; she's not made some type of irrevocable decision. She can certainly take additional withdrawals from these accounts, although it will reduce her guaranteed income proportionally. So, there is some flexibility.

Again, it's not right for everyone, but this type of sequential income planning can work very nicely because you're not depending on the stock market performance for income.

BENEFICIARY DESIGNATIONS

Regardless of when you're working, if your money is in TSP, make sure when you retire that you complete form TSP-3 to name beneficiaries. If you're not sure whether you've done that, just submit another form, because the new form will preempt your old one. Make sure, too, that you keep a copy of that new TSP-3 on hand.

One piece of wording you'll see on this TSP-3 form bothers me; it says that if you're married and you fail to list your spouse as the beneficiary, they're going to get the money regardless. Now, this is true – but it's much simpler if there is a designated beneficiary on file. A problem that could occur is when your spouse gets the payout, if he/she doesn't have the financial savvy to do a 60-day rollover into their own IRA, they're going to pay income taxes on it. If you're looking at a large TSP being paid out and classified as income in a single year, your spouse will lose a hefty chunk of that money to taxes.

So always, always, always name beneficiaries; name your primary beneficiaries, and name contingents. It's the easiest, most simple form of estate planning you can do. Again, if there are no beneficiaries designated on your TSP, it will go in the order of precedence; number one, it'll go to the widow or widower, and if there is none, it will go to your child or children equally, and to the descendants of your deceased children by representation. If you have no children, it will go to the parents equally or to the surviving parent, and if there is none, it will go to the executor or administrator of the estate.

OVERALL ACTION STEPS
FOR YOUR THRIFT SAVINGS PLAN

Number one, you need to determine your goal. How do you know what your goal should be? There is a calculator on the TSP.gov website that can help you determine how much you need to save to get to whatever your specific goal is, and certainly you need to have an income goal overall.

Believe it or not, as I meet with federal employees, the hardest question for them to answer is, what is your desired monthly net income? We're talking here about net income after taxes, in today's dollars, during retirement. It always surprises me that, no matter to whom I'm talking, or what grade and step level they are or what age, time and time again, I hear, "Well, gee, I haven't really thought about that." That's a critical piece of your retirement planning. Just being eligible for retirement isn't enough; you need to be sure you're financially able to retire, that you have the income you'll need, and how much specifically you'll need to take from your Thrift Savings Plan.

So have a goal. With that goal, you need to know what your savings rate is, and adjust that in order to successfully meet your goal. And just as important as it is to know how much you need to save, of equal importance is how is your portfolio is allocated. What's your strategy for getting that necessary return from your TSP?

Create a diversification strategy that takes into account your risk tolerance. Think about that; how much potential loss can you stomach? You know that if you have managed to save $200,000 in your TSP and it's in the C Fund, historically that fund has done very well. But if it takes a hit and has a 30 percent decline, can you live with losing $60,000? Ask yourself that question, look at your investment horizon, and answer it honestly.

Certainly if you're further away from retirement, you'll potentially have the opportunity to make up losses in your portfolio. Again, look at your goals - your income goals and other goals that you may have - and determine your process for managing your TSP. Are you going to leave it in TSP, and if so, what is your strategy for allocating it? Are you going to manage it yourself? Are you going to work with a financial advisor? If you're going to do that, I would certainly recommend that you choose one who is educated in the federal benefits arena, so they know the ins and outs of what you can and can't do. And take advantage of the resources that provide guidance for allocation strategies. My favorite resource for TSP strategies is what we mentioned earlier, www.MyTSPVision.com. There are others out there, too, and you need to be aware of what's available.

Certainly, perform ongoing maintenance on your account. We're not talking about just opening up the envelope and looking at your balance; you need to do something called rebalancing. For instance, say that your ideal portfolio allocation is to have 50% in the C Fund and 50% in the G Fund. If we go through a bull market, now that C Fund has gotten up to 60% of your portfolio, so you'll need to go back and rebalance your portfolio to where you wanted it to be, at 50/50. Probably once a year would be a good schedule for rebalancing.

And while you're doing that, it's also a good time for you to reassess your risk tolerance, whether it's while you're still working, close to retirement, or during retirement. Reassess how much risk you can take; consider what you're comfortable with. Certainly, look at the outside environment to determine if you want to make changes based on the markets, the economy, and what's going on in our country as well as globally, to determine if you're comfortable with the amount of risk that you're taking.

Again, have a plan, and follow it – but allow for adjustments that are going to arise from life changes along the way.

[1] Past market performance is no guarantee of future investment performance or success Your results will vary.

[2] Asset Allocation and diversification do not ensure a profit or guarantee against loss: they are methods to manage risk.

[3] This example and rates of return are for illustrative purposes only and are not indicative of future investment returns. Please consult with a qualified professional before making investment decisions.

[4] A fixed indexed annuity is not an investment in the "'market" or in the applicable index: the participation rate and/or cap rate, and any other non-guaranteed components of the indexing formula may change and may be different in the future; Disclose that the indexed interest could be less than with a traditional product, and could be zero (if applicable); Some indexed annuities guarantee a minimum interest rate.

Indexed annuities may not be suitable for all investors. Features such as participation rates, rate caps, and spread/asset/margin fees may change over time and adversely affect your return if an insurance company subsequently lowers the participation rate or cap or increases the spread/asset/margin fees.

Some fixed annuities come with high guaranteed interest rates that can decrease after a set number of years to a much lower minimal interest rate.

Investors can lose principal if an indexed annuity is terminated prior to the end of the surrender period.

The principal guarantee and income for life guarantee features of fixed and indexed annuities arc subject to the claims-paying ability of the issuing insurance company.

If you take an early distribution from an annuity you may be subject to a surrender charge, which could result in a loss of principal. You may also be subject to a tax penalty if you make a withdrawal before age 59.

SECTION

3

LIFE, HEALTH, AND LONG TERM CARE; FEHB, FEGLI, AND FLTCIP

AN INTRODUCTION

---- ★ ----

While you as a federal employee have some of the greatest insurance benefits, they can be pretty confusing. First off you need to learn a different language. Life insurance is FEGLI, health insurance programs are referred to as FEHB, and the acronym for your long-term care insurance plan is FLTCIP. Now that you know the language, specifically what are the benefits, what do they cost, what do they do, and what do they mean? This chapter will explain how these programs work, what they cost, and guide you in determining what are the most beneficial programs for you and your family.

My cousin has worked for NASA for 20 years. During a conversation he told me that he did not have life insurance coverage at work, and someone in his agency had told him he absolutely could not get it. I told him that he most certainly could apply, but would have to go through underwriting, and a decision would be made based on his health. I emailed him SF 2817, which he completed and turned in to his agency. A month later, he had FEGLI basic life insurance!

Most feds mistakenly believe that if they didn't elect to sign up for life insurance when they first were employed or during an Open Season, they are not eligible. This is not true. You can still apply for coverage but you must go through underwriting.

CHAPTER 5

FEDERAL EMPLOYEE HEALTH BENEFIT – FEHB

———————— ⭐ ————————

One of the most intimidating things to do is make a change to your health insurance. Why? Because the health insurance plan documents are 160 pages long, and the thought of going through 10 of these is exhausting. The good news is that OPM requires each document to follow the same format with the information in the same sections in each plan. Even if you are happy with your health insurance, each year during Open Season, you should at least look at Section 2, which tells you of any changes to the plan for the coming year.

The worksheets in this chapter are designed to simplify the process of choosing the best healthcare plan for you and your family. They are geared to getting you to think about what is important to you in a plan, and how to narrow down to a few plans that meet your objectives. Then you can look at the plan documents, go to the plan websites and call and speak to a representative from the insurance company.

FEHB is the second-best benefit that you receive as a result of being a federal employee, the first being your pension. While you're working, your share of the premiums for health insurance is paid using what's known as premium conversion, or pretax dollars. Many federal employees believe that their share of the premium goes up when they retire. This is not true. They continue to pay approximately 28% of the premium with approximately 72% of the premium being subsidized by the federal government.

Even though you are still paying the same proportion, it will feel as if your premium goes up in retirement. In retirement, you must pay your premiums with after-tax dollars instead of pretax dollars. If you do three things, you can take your FEHB with you into retirement:

- You have to be insured on the day of your retirement.
- You have to retire on an immediate annuity. In other words, you have to start taking your pension right away.
- You have to have been enrolled or covered as a family member for the five years immediately preceding your retirement or since your first opportunity to enroll.

Five years doesn't mean four years and 364 days. It means five years. I have a client who was covered under her husband's insurance. When she got within five years of retirement, during FEHB Open Season, she signed up for coverage. She thought, "Okay, everything's fine because I'm not retiring until the end of the December – five years from now." However, that year her insurance took effect on January 4th which meant technically she'd only given the plan four years and

361 days when she went to retire five years later. On December 31, when she wanted to retire, she ended up having to work another month until the end of January to have the full five years. If you are enrolling in FEHB at the end of your career in order to take health insurance with you into retirement, make sure you enroll in time to have five full years of enrollment prior to retirement.

You have many great choices for plans. Every year, there's an Open Season, which is typically conducted from the second Tuesday in November through the second Tuesday in December. During this Open Season, you can enroll in, cancel, or change your health plan. There is a "no pre-existing condition" clause, which means that you can move from one plan to the next, and they're never going to ask you, "Did you have a bad health incident this past year? Is that why you're switching insurance?" OPM requires all carriers to allow their participants to move from plan to plan each year.

Depending on where you live, you will be able to choose between some local plans in your area. You'll also be able to choose between six national plans that are available to every federal employee in the United States. As you look at choosing a health plan, you're going to choose how you want that healthcare provided. In other words, what type of insurance might make sense for you?

You might choose a health maintenance organization, or HMO. In this type of plan, you typically choose a primary care physician from a list of physicians that's provided to you. That primary care physician provides all your general medical care, and they have to provide you with a referral to see a specialist. The big thing to remember about an HMO is that there is no coverage for out-of-network care. You have to stay in their service area. You typically don't pay any deductible with an HMO, but members usually pay a copay when they receive care from their physician. HMOs typically have a lower premium cost. So the tradeoff if you decide to go with an HMO is that you have less choice, but you get to pay less.

In your area, you may also have something known as a preferred provider organization ("PPO"), and in that case you don't have to choose a primary care physician as long as you choose to go to a physician that's on their preferred provider list; thus the PPO designation. You can go to any physician on that list, and change doctors whenever you wish.

You can refer yourself to your own specialist. You don't have to stay within network, and it still will cover some of your costs. However, you have a financial incentive to stay in network because the insurance company will pay more. In a PPO, you typically will have a deductible before your benefits begin, and there also will be a copay for each visit that you have to a healthcare facility. This tends to be a little more costly than an HMO in terms of premiums because you have more choices.

Finally, we have the fee-for-service plans that are available to all federal employees across the United States. These are very similar to the PPO in that you choose the doctor or the hospital within the provider network. One difference between the fee-for-service and the PPO is you only receive a reimbursement for the covered medical expenses listed in your policy, which is typically about 80% of "reasonable and customary." You may find that there is a discrepancy between what the doctor thinks is usual and customary and what the insurance company thinks is usual and customary.

The six insurance companies that fall under the national fee-for-service category available to all federal employees are APWU, Blue Cross/Blue Shield, GEHA, Mail Handlers, NALC, and Samba.

Once you decide how much choice you will have in the selection of your physician or where the care is delivered, you're going to go to the next level within that plan to decide if you want a traditional plan, a consumer-driven health plan, or a high-deductible health plan. Consumer-driven and high-deductible health plans have been offered since 2006, so there's not a lot of utilization of these plans. That doesn't mean it's not a great option for you. If you choose a traditional plan, you're going to then choose one more level of care: high, standard, basic, or value. Keep in mind that not every traditional plan offers all four of these levels of service.

For example, Blue Cross/Blue Shield offers only a traditional plan in levels of Standard or Basic, with the Standard being more costly, offering a few more bells and whistles, and the Basic being less expensive. We know that more federal employees utilize Blue Cross/ Blue Shield than any other plan. Does this mean that Blue Cross/ Blue Shield is the best choice for everyone? There's a good possibility that the reason so many people are in Blue Cross/Blue Shield is that it has a national network of providers. It has been around a long time, and many federal employees make their healthcare choice simply by going into the break room, finding someone who looks smart and asking, "What do you have? It's Open Season. Help me decide." If you do your research a little more thoroughly, Open Season is a great opportunity for you to possibly save some money and certainly to get coverage that's a good fit for you.

We tend to look at choosing a health plan by simply looking at the premiums and not considering our overall healthcare costs. If you are in, for example, a PPO or a fee-for-service plan, you're probably paying a fairly high premium. You stand to have a lot of things covered and paid for, but if you're really healthy and you don't use any of those benefits, you're paying too much for your premiums. You could pay a lower premium and have the same results and benefits, and pay less for your overall healthcare. It's important that you think in terms of overall healthcare costs as opposed to just looking at premiums.

When you're comparing a traditional plan, a consumer-driven plan, and a high-deductible health plan, and trying to make the best choice for your plan among these three options, you're asking yourself, "How healthy am I, and how healthy are my family members who are covered by my FEHB?" A traditional plan is for people who have more significant, ongoing medical issues. If you anticipate multiple visits with a specialist, if you have ongoing prescription needs, and you take two or three prescription medications every month, you may want to look at a traditional plan. It includes higher premiums, but it typically will have lower deductibles and lower copays. It'll have an annual out-of-pocket limit (which all FEHB plans are required to have), which means that at some point when you reach that spending threshold, you're not going to pay any more that year out of your own pocket.

The consumer-driven health plan ("CDHP") was introduced to federal employees in 2006 and only about 2% of federal employees have joined the plan. I believe this is because federal employees don't tend to be pioneers. They are more likely to hang back, send someone else in and see if they come back alive. Even though the consumer-driven health plan has been around for five years, federal employees still are waiting to ask a co-worker, "Okay, you tried it. How did that go?"

A consumer-driven health plan is for those who generally are healthy with minor, ongoing medical needs. You may have seasonal allergies or something like acid reflux. If you need any specialist visits during the year, it would be anticipated that you would only need one. Of course, the state of your health can always change during the year, but that's really your whole risk as you make your election in Open Season. You could have a health change during the year, but you're only required to stay in that health plan for one year. You could go to another plan that more closely meets your needs in the following Open Season.

If you have few prescription needs, a consumer-driven health plan can be fairly attractive. It sets up an account that works as a reverse deductible; for example, your plan might say that the first $2,000 of your expenses will be paid for by the insurance company. You would have no deductibles and no copays for the first $2,000 of expenses. After that, your deductible and your copays would kick in. If you didn't use more than $2,000 in a year, you wouldn't pay anything out of your own pocket (other than your premiums). If you didn't use all of that money, the funds roll over from year to year as long as you stay with the same insurer. If you only spent $1,500 of the insurance company's money this year, then you'd have $500 to roll over and the next year, they'd pay the first $2,500 worth of care.

A CDHP lets you pay lower premiums than a traditional plan; it still has your maximum annual out-of-pocket limits and, if you're fairly healthy, it can be a great way to manage your healthcare costs.

The high deductible health plan ("HDHP") is for those who have no known medical issues. You may have a routine visit such as an annual physical, or develop the flu and go to the doctor, or fall during a hike and break your ankle - but if you typically don't see a physician other than in those kinds of cases and you have no ongoing prescription medication, a high deductible health plan might be a great option for you. The big benefit of the HDHP is that it includes a health savings account ("HSA") that can be rolled over from year to year. It's one step beyond what you get in the consumer-driven health plan, because these "saved" healthcare dollars are actually yours to spend any time in your lifetime. It acts like a healthcare IRA. You have lower premiums – sometimes significantly lower premiums – than a traditional or a consumer-driven health plan.

Looking at the health savings account, it is the largest benefit of being in a high deductible health plan. In a high deductible health plan, you're going to have some minimum deductibles that you have to pay before any of your benefits are paid. Think about the old catastrophic policies where people would say, "I can pay for my doctor's visits, I can pay for my prescriptions, but if I have to have open heart surgery, I want a safety net, I want somebody to help me." That's how an HDHP works.

This HSA in a high deductible health plan allows you to save pretax dollars for future medical expenses. You own the account. When we talk about a high deductible health plan being less expensive, there are two ways that you get money into your health savings account. You can put money in up to an annual limit, and the insurance company also makes a contribution on your behalf that's really a rebate of your premiums.

If you look at the premiums for high deductible health plans on the OPM website, you might say, "They're less expensive but they're not that much less expensive." In order to get the whole picture, you need to go to the outline of coverage and look at the reimbursement clause. What that will tell you is how much of that premium is going to be refunded or come back to you as a rebate directly into your health savings account. You can then use your HSA to pay your deductible if, heaven forbid, you do need healthcare during the year that you didn't anticipate. You also are building a way in which you can have pretax healthcare dollars for the future, throughout your lifetime, so it's a nice way to maximize your health coverage for people who are healthy. If you know you have ongoing medical conditions, the HDHP may not be the best choice for you.

During Open Season, although it is not technically a part of the FEHB plan, you're also allowed to create a flexible savings account. You can set aside up to $5,000 a year in pretax dollars to pay for medical costs, deductibles, and copays. You can also set aside up to $5,000 a year in pretax dollars to pay for dependent care. This might include elder care if you have parents living with you who can't be left alone while you go to work.

Keep in mind that in 2013 the FSA allowable amount goes to $2,500 a year for medical costs. The other big change we've seen to the FSA is that you are no longer allowed to be reimbursed out of this account for nonprescription drugs and medications. If your physician is willing to write you a prescription for Tylenol PM, you can pay for it out of your FSA.

The one big disadvantage of the FSA is that it's "use it or lose it." The rules of the plan require you to utilize your FSA by March 15th of the following year, so you have to make a plan about how you're going use this FSA.

Another common complaint is that it involves a lot of paperwork; you have to file the claim for reimbursement. That has gotten easier and easier each year. Many insurance companies will actually file with your FSA for you, and the money is deposited directly into your bank account. They're trying to make the process simpler for you.

In addition to the consumer-driven and high-deductible health plans, dental and vision programs were added back in 2006. The premiums are not subsidized by the federal government. The federal employee or the retiree is responsible for the full amount of premiums, but those premiums are reasonable, because you're taking advantage of being a member of a huge group of people who has access to it. It is purchased on a group basis on your behalf, but you're going to pay the entire premium.

★ ★

Pre-existing conditions are included in dental and vision coverage when you enroll in or change from one plan to another, but what you need to ask before you switch is when. There is typically a two-year wait for a pre-existing condition such as orthodontics to be covered within the dental programs.

As an example, your son or daughter needs braces this year, so you decide, "Hey, this is the year I'm going to sign up for some dental coverage to get some help with that orthodontist."

You sign up for it. You take them to the orthodontist and when your claim is submitted the insurance company says, "Oh, you have to have been covered for two years before we cover orthodontics." Yes, pre-existing conditions are covered and certainly, if their teeth are still crooked two years from now, you'll be able to go and have them pay some portion of those orthodontics. You have to be aware of when you might need to get in the plan.

★ ★

You can take just dental or just vision. You can take both. You can take neither. You can move in and out of these plans in any given year. You can never have had either one of them while you were working, and then decide to get them while you're retired. Anything goes; it's much more flexible because the federal government isn't paying any portion of the premium. You don't have to have been enrolled for five years prior to retirement in order to have that access or eligibility in retirement.

CHAPTER
6

FEDERAL EMPLOYEES'
GROUP LIFE INSURANCE –
FEGLI

---　★　---

L et's look at the Federal Employees' Group Life Insurance ("FEGLI") next. You must have Basic Coverage in order to have anything else. Your Basic Coverage is your current salary rounded to the nearest thousand, plus $2,000. The federal government pays one-third of the premium, helping to keep the premiums reasonable. The employee pays two-thirds of the premium, or 15 cents per thousand, and the cost of this coverage doesn't go up based on the employee's age. The only time your basic insurance costs go up is if you receive a raise or a promotion that causes you to have a higher salary, which results in your coverage increasing.

This option is the least expensive of the Federal Employees' Group Life Insurance coverage. When you come to work for the federal government, if you are under age 35, you actually get double the basic benefit. You get your current salary rounded to the nearest thousand plus $2,000, plus one more multiple of your salary that you don't have to pay for. The current provider of FEGLI is Metropolitan Life, and Metropolitan Life throws that in as a little gift for young federal employees.

You're probably wondering, "How can they afford to do that?" You're not going be under 35 forever, and the odds are in Met Life's favor that you're not going to pass away. Once you reach age 35, your benefits start to reduce by 10% a year until at age 45, that double benefit is completely gone.

You must have Basic Coverage to have any of the other three options, but once you have Basic Coverage you can elect to have:

- Option A, which is a flat $10,000 in addition to your Basic Coverage. The costs for this vary, because it is based on your age and no portion of it is subsidized by the federal government.
- Option B is the most expensive option within FEGLI. It is your current salary, rounded to the nearest thousand. You can have multiples from one through five of that amount. You could have up to six times your salary if you had Basic plus five multiples of Option B.

The cost of Option B coverage goes up every time you have a birthday that ends in a zero or a five (age 50, 55 and 60). Many federal employees elected this coverage when they first came to work for the government. They were in their 20s, it was inexpensive coverage, so it made sense. "I might as well buy as much as I can. I don't have to qualify by going through underwriting. I'll just take a lot of coverage." Time passes; all of a sudden you have your 50th birthday, and you see this big number coming out of your check, and you're wondering, "What in the world happened?" It's your Option B life insurance premiums.

The chart shows what the cost per thousand is, and it gives us a very clear example of how those premiums increase with your age:

Age Band	Premium/$1000/Month
For persons ages 35 and under	$0.065
For persons ages 35 through 39	$0.087
For persons ages 40 through 44	$0.13
For persons ages 45 through 49	$0.195
For persons ages 50 through 54	$0.303
For persons ages 55 through 59	$0.607
For persons ages 60 through 64	$1.30
For persons ages 65 through 69	$1.56
For persons ages 70 through 74	$2.60
For persons ages 75 through 79	$3.90
For persons ages 80 & Over	$5.20

This chart reflects keeping the full Option B life insurance coverage during retirement.

Option C, the final option, allows you to cover your spouse or your minor children. You can cover your spouse in multiples of $5,000, and you can buy multiples of one through five of that. You can cover your children up to the age of 22, in multiples of 1 through

5 of $2,500 for each child. These costs only increase for the federal employee with his or her age. They don't look at the age of the spouse that you're covering or the children, just the employee's age.

In retirement, you decide how much of your FEGLI you're going to keep.

Most federal employees choose to keep their basic coverage with a 75 percent reduction, and they eliminate their other coverage. This reduces or eliminates the cost at age 65. The following example illustrates a common scenario.

Your life insurance coverage includes: Basic (equal to your rounded annual salary plus $2000). You plan to retire at the age of 58. You elected to reduce your Basic coverage by 2% monthly to 25% of full Basic Coverage beginning at the age of 65.

FEGLI Premiums and Coverage

Age Annual	Salary	Biweekly Premium	Monthly Premium	Annual Premium	Accumulated Cost	Basic Option	Option A	Option B	Option C	Total Coverage
56/57	54,124	8.55	18.53	222	222	57,000	0	0	0	57,000
57/58	54,124	8.55	18.53	222	445	57,000	0	0	0	57,000
58/59	0	8.55	18.53	222	667	57,000	0	0	0	57,000
59/60	0	8.55	18.53	222	889	57,000	0	0	0	57,000
60/61	0	8.55	18.53	222	1,112	57,000	0	0	0	57,000
61/62	0	8.55	18.53	222	1,334	57,000	0	0	0	57,000
62/63	0	8.55	18.53	222	1,556	57,000	0	0	0	57,000
63/64	0	8.55	18.53	222	1,778	57,000	0	0	0	57,000
64/65	0	8.55	18.53	222	2,001	57,000	0	0	0	57,000
65/66	0	0	0	0	2,001	57,000	0	0	0	57,000
66/67	0	0	0	0	2,001	43,320	0	0	0	43,320
67/68	0	0	0	0	2,001	29,640	0	0	0	29,640
68/69	0	0	0	0	2,001	15,960	0	0	0	15,960
69/70	0	0	0	0	2,001	14,250	0	0	0	14,250

CHAPTER 7

FEDERAL LONG TERM CARE INSURANCE PROGRAM – FLTCIP

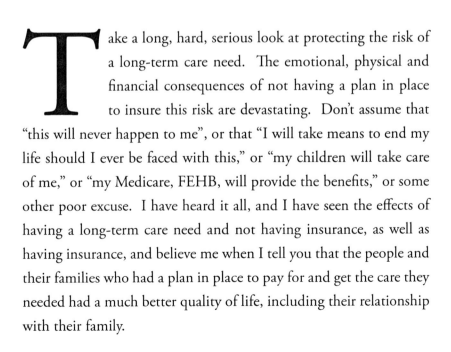

Take a long, hard, serious look at protecting the risk of a long-term care need. The emotional, physical and financial consequences of not having a plan in place to insure this risk are devastating. Don't assume that "this will never happen to me", or that "I will take means to end my life should I ever be faced with this," or "my children will take care of me," or "my Medicare, FEHB, will provide the benefits," or some other poor excuse. I have heard it all, and I have seen the effects of having a long-term care need and not having insurance, as well as having insurance, and believe me when I tell you that the people and their families who had a plan in place to pay for and get the care they needed had a much better quality of life, including their relationship with their family.

FLTCIP is the longest acronym in federal benefits. The people at Long Term Care Partners, administrator of the federal plan, pronounce it "flitsip." This is Federal Long Term Care Insurance Program 2.0, meaning this is version two. The original started in 2002 and was renewed in 2009.

John Hancock and MetLife were awarded the original contract. When the contract was renewed, John Hancock was awarded the contract for the second seven-year period. To this point, there has only been an Open Season for these benefits when the contract renews, so it's not a frequent occurrence. Open Season is great for those federal employees who wish to look at long-term care and have some health issues that might prevent them from getting private coverage. The Federal Long Term Care Program is available to current employees, their spouses or same-sex partners, and retirees and their spouses or same-sex partner. During Open Season, coverage is offered to current employees on a limited underwriting basis. This allows them to qualify by answering fewer questions on the application.

When you're choosing long-term care coverage, you make four choices. You choose how much a day you want your long-term care coverage to pay. You choose how long a period you want it to cover once you start using benefits. You choose how much inflation protection you want. We know that the cost of long-term care is going up at least as fast as the cost of healthcare, so you want make sure that the benefits you have inside your long-term care insurance will grow to keep up with those costs. You're also going choose your deductible. This is how long you'll pay out-of-pocket for your care before the insurance company starts paying benefits.

You have the election on how much your benefit is going to cover. You can choose anywhere from $100 a day to $500 a day in $50 increments, so you could choose $150 a day, $200 a day, $250 a day, etc. In figuring out what you'll need, look at what the costs of care are for your local area, and remember that you don't necessarily need long-term care insurance to cover the entire cost of your care. You just want to make sure that you don't immediately have to run to your own assets and start withdrawing them.

You will continue to have a pension as long as you're living. If you are collecting your annuity and you need long-term care, chances are that some of your other expenses, like travel or golf, will be curtailed, so some of that money can go toward paying for long-term care. Your insurance will supplement that.

When you elect how long you want it to pay, you get to choose two years, three years, five years, or lifetime. The average length of stay for a patient in long- term care statistically is two and a half years, so a two-year, three-year, or five-year plan, depending also on your family history, might be a good election for you.

The most expensive option is lifetime coverage, because the insurance company doesn't know how long they might have to pay. It's very hard for them to quantify that risk. Inflation protection is something you want make sure that you add to this coverage, since the cost of long-term care is increasing rapidly, and you want to make sure that your benefits are keeping up with those rising costs.

The deductible in long-term care has a really bad name. The marketing department at the insurance company must have been out that day. They were trying to figure out what to call this deductible, so they named it the "elimination period." If you have not been eliminated after 90 days, then your long-term care insurance is going to kick in. Think of it as a deductible that is measured in days instead of dollars.

You only have one choice for this deductible in the federal plan and that's 90 days. That means you're going to pay for the first 90 days of your care, before your insurance begins paying the daily benefit. If your own physician certifies that he expects you to need care for at least 90 days, and you need assistance with two out of six activities of daily living – bathing, dressing, feeding yourself, toileting, incontinence, and transferring (being able to get out of a chair and moving from place to place on your own) – you will be eligible to start collecting your long-term care insurance. A diagnosis of Alzheimer's or dementia will also trigger the qualification for benefits, even in the absence of any of the other triggers.

The statistics tell us that about 50% of the population who reach age 65 will need long-term care at some point in their lifetimes. It's kind of a roll of the dice; half of the population will need care and half of it won't.

If you are healthy today, if you are married, if you live in a state where you might be offered discounts like those available from AAA, it could make a lot of sense for you to investigate private long-term care coverage, because there's a good chance that you can get richer benefits for a lower premium by looking into those outside plans.

SECTION

4

ENTITLEMENTS SOCIAL SECURITY AND MEDICARE

AN INTRODUCTION

———————— ★ ————————

Our country's entitlement programs are endangered. As of this writing, the combined unfunded entitlement obligations are $46 trillion. (The White House, US Treasury.) Fifteen Trillion is the unfunded liability of Social Security, with the remaining liability coming from Medicare and Medicaid.

In 2016, Social Security will begin paying more in benefits than they collect in taxes. Without changes, by 2036 the Social Security Trust Fund will be exhausted, and there will be enough money to pay only about 76 cents for each dollar of scheduled benefits. (socialsecurity.gov)

The first of the baby boomers turned 65 in January 2011. All boomers will turn 65 by 2030, at which time 18% of the US population will be 65+; an all time high! The 2011 Medicare Trustees Report has projected that the hospital portion of Medicare will be exhausted in 2024. This statement is certainly cause for worries among baby boomers.

Many boomers are asking questions such as:

- Will Social Security be means-tested?
- Will Medicare be rationed?

Despite all the heated political talk about Medicare and Social Security, the reality is that Washington cannot ignore the problem. While it is impossible to predict the changes that may occur with Social Security and Medicare, this chapter deals with what you can expect from these programs at the present time.

CHAPTER 8

SOCIAL SECURITY

———————————— ★ ————————————

When it comes to "When should I take Social Security?" if you're eligible, the big concern is that we don't know how long you're going to live. If that was something we could quantify accurately, then we could determine the best time to take Social Security and whether you should wait or not. However, we don't get to know that. We have another complicating factor, in that we're becoming more and more concerned about the viability of Social Security and its ability to pay the full benefits that have been promised to you. That too is an issue that we need to consider in deciding when to take Social Security. Ultimately, it's an individual decision, and in this chapter we'll walk through some of the things that Baby Boomers want to know: Will Social Security be there for me? How much can I expect to receive? When should I apply? How can I maximize my benefits? And will Social Security be enough to live on in retirement?

Most of us realize that the answer to that last question is "no" – Social Security alone won't be adequate to fund your retirement. Having said that, most people tend to minimize the value of Social Security, especially given the current economic environment and fears about Social Security being underfunded. While they understand that they are likely to get something back from this system, they think it's going to be a minimal amount and not really enough to count on.

However, Social Security is much more valuable than a lot of people realize. If the past is any indication, people who are retiring today, or even within ten years, probably are not going to be affected by the likely changes to Social Security in the future.

Social Security provides income you can't outlive. If your monthly benefit is $2,000 and you live for 10 years, you're going to receive a total of $240,000 in benefits. If you live for 20 years, you're going to receive a total of $480,000 in benefits. If you're fortunate enough to live 30 years in retirement, Social Security is going to pay you $720,000 in benefits. And that's not taking into account COLA adjustments, which have historically averaged 2.8% a year. A monthly benefit today of $2,000 with annual COLAs of 2.8%, would be $2,636 after 10 years, and $3,474, after 20 years.

Social Security also offers survivor benefits; while those spouses are living, if they've paid into Social Security, they're entitled to Social Security benefits. After one spouse dies, the remaining spouse is entitled to the higher of either one of their benefits.

Let's talk about Question No. 1: Will Social Security be there for me? According to the trustees from Social Security, the trust fund is on target to be depleted in 2036. Right now, Social Security has an unfunded liability of $15 trillion. In 2016, we'll begin to pay more in benefits than we collect in taxes. So, without changes, by 2036 the Social Security Trust Fund will be exhausted. There will only be enough money to pay out about 78¢ for each dollar of scheduled benefits.

According to the 2010 Trustee's Report, the Social Security Trust Fund now holds about $2.5 trillion in reserves. These reserve funds are invested in specially issued US Treasury securities, and they would be available for paying benefits should revenues fall short of expenses. In 2084, if it remains on its current course, they'll only be able to cover 75% of the benefits that are to be paid out.

Social Security and Medicare entitlement programs represent 8.4% of our annual nation's economy. That's expected to increase to 11.8% by 2035. We mentioned above that 2036 is when Social Security is set to run out of trust funds, which is one year sooner than last year's projection. To fully fund future needs, it would need 14.62% in payroll taxes. Currently, the combined payroll tax from employees and employer is 12.4%.

What are some ways to restore solvency to the system? Some of the solutions proposed have included, first, to increase the maximum earnings subject to Social Security tax, which is currently $106,800. Currently, anyone earning over that does not have to continue to pay into Social Security tax on earnings above that amount. A second proposal is to raise the normal full retirement age, which currently is age 66 for individuals born between 1943 and 1954, or 67 for those born in 1960 or later.

Another proposal is to lower benefits for future retirees, and to escalate benefits based on increases in consumer prices rather than wages. The last proposal of which I'm aware is to reduce the cost of living adjustments for all retirees. That's pretty scary, because federal employees rely on cost of living adjustments, not only in Social

Security but in their pensions as well, so this could have a sizable negative impact.

How much can you expect to receive? We've established that we're pretty comfortable that it's going to be there; at least, some of it. Your benefits are going to depend on how much you earn over your working career, and the age at which you apply for benefits. Social Security is calculated by a formula that includes your highest 35 years of earnings. If you had any missing years, they count as zeros. Your earnings are indexed for inflation and averaged, which becomes your AIME, or your Average Indexed Monthly Earnings. Then this formula is applied to your AIME to determine your primary insurance amount, (PIA). This is the amount you'll receive at full retirement age.

Example of Social Security benefit formula
- Baby Boomer born in 1946
- Maximum Social Security earnings every year since age 22
- AIME = $7,260
- PIA formula:

$749 x .90 =	714.60
$3,768 x .32 =	1,205.76
$2,743 x .15 =	411.45
Total	$2,331.81
PIA = $2,331.81	

Amount worker will receive at full retirement age (66)

What if you apply for early benefits? Typically, the average age for a federal employee to retire is somewhere between 57 and 62, so should you begin taking Social Security at age 62? There is a lot of discussion that maybe you should, because it might not be there for you if you wait.

But let's look at that comparison. Let's say you applied at age 62 and, for the purposes of this example, you were born somewhere between 1943 and 1954. If you apply at 62, you'll only get 75% of your full retirement benefit, which means that if your benefit is $2,230, 75% of that is $1,672.00. By applying at 62, you're giving up 25% of your benefit permanently.

What happens if you apply after your full retirement age? Using the example of full retirement age being 66, and assuming that Social Security payment is $2,230, what happens if you delay your credits and don't apply until you're 70, which is the maximum age that you can delay them? Even if there's no cost of living, you'll get a 32% increase by delaying those four years. That's an 8% average increase by delaying and waiting until age 70. Again, that's assuming that we don't have any cost of living increase.

Why else might you delay benefits, aside from that 32% increase? Well, historically the average increase for Social Security in COLAs has been 2.8 percent, which actually ends up being an increase of 16 percent per year. In today's environment, where can you go and get an investment that's going to give you a guaranteed 8%, or possibly a 16%, increase each year?

So, what you want to consider is, do I have another asset from which I can carve out this income and delay taking Social Security?

You can do the math; start by looking at your Social Security statement to make sure that it's accurate. Go to www.socialsecurity. gov, and click on "estimate your retirement benefits." You'll need your Social Security number and your mother's maiden name to access your records, and it will estimate your benefits for you.

Let's talk next about spousal benefits. Spousal benefits entitle a spouse, to half the primary worker's benefits. Let's say, for example, that John's benefit is $2,000. Because of his wife Jane's work history, her benefit is only $800. Jane is entitled to the higher of either half of her spouse's benefits, or her own benefit. In this case, her spousal benefit is higher and would be $1,000.

There are some rules to remember for spousal benefits and they are:

- The spouse will receive the higher of his or her own benefit or the spousal benefit.
- The primary worker must have applied for benefits, but they can suspend to build delayed credits if they're over their full retirement age. That can be a great strategy, as we'll explain below.
- The spouse must be at least 62 for reduced benefit, or 66 for a full benefit.
- There are no delayed credits on a spousal benefit after the age of 66. So if the spouse says, "I'm going to delay getting my credits, past my full retirement age of 66," the spousal benefit is not going to increase like it would if it was your own benefits.

There are also Social Security benefits for a divorced spouse, which is the same as the spousal benefit, if the marriage lasted for 10 years or more and if the person who received the divorced spouse benefits is currently unmarried. You can have more than one ex-spouse receiving benefits on the same worker's record. Benefits paid to one ex-spouse do not affect those paid to the worker, the current spouse, or other ex-spouses. The worker will not even be notified that the ex-spouse has applied for benefits.

Social Security also includes survivor's benefits, so when one spouse dies, the surviving spouse receives the higher of the two benefits. Example No. 1: Jack and Sarah are married. Jack's benefit is $2,000: Sarah's benefit is $1,200. Jack dies. Sarah notifies Social Security, and her $1,200 benefit is automatically replaced with her $2,000 survivor benefit. If Sarah were the one to die, Jack would retain his $2,000 benefit. There are rules for survivor benefits; the couple must be legally married, a man and woman. Same-sex marriages are not recognized, although common-law marriages are recognized in some instances.

You must have been married for at least nine months at the date of death. There's an exception in the case of accidents. The survivor must be at least 60 to receive a reduced benefit, unless they're disabled; if they are disabled, they can begin receiving that benefit at age 50. A divorced spouse survivor benefit is available if the marriage lasted at least 10 years.

Let's move on and dig deeper into the question, when should I apply for benefits? There's not any clear-cut rule, but some factors to consider when deciding when to apply are:

- What's your health status?
- What's your life expectancy?
- What's your need for income?
- Do you plan to continue to work?
- What are your survivor needs?

Typically, the break-even analysis for delaying benefits to your full retirement age, versus taking them at age 62, is about age 77. The break-even for delaying and starting the benefits at age 70 goes up to about age 80. So it can definitely be beneficial to delay benefits if you believe that you're healthy and you're going to live until at least age 80.

The key point to remember when applying for Social Security is that if you apply early, your benefit starts lower and stays lower for life. It's not going to go up when you reach age 66. COLA magnified the impact to early or delayed retirement. The longer your life, the more beneficial it is to delay benefits. This decision impacts not only your benefits, but your survivor benefits as well. Delaying benefits will give the survivor more income.

Are there ways to maximize Social Security benefits legally? The answer is, yes. If they're available, there's no reason why you shouldn't maximize your benefits. How? One way is to improve your earnings record. Examine your earnings record from your latest Social Security Statement to determine if it's accurate. Are you missing any years? Can you improve it by working longer?

In examining your Social Security Statement, double-check to make sure that all of the years that you've worked are accounted for and correct. If you discover that your work history is inaccurate on your statement, you have to take steps to insure that it's corrected.

★ ★

About two years ago, a federal employee and his wife came to visit me. He was outraged that he had 12 years missing from his Social Security statement. He told me that for the two to three years before he had met with me, he'd been chasing his tail trying to figure out a way to get his work history corrected on his Social Security. A significant amount of money that he paid in was not showing. He had changed agencies during his career, and the first agency told him that it was the second agency's responsibility. The second agency told him that he had to go to Social Security and work it out there – but in fact it really was the responsibility of that particular agency to make sure that his benefits were paid in.

✴ ✴

There is a special agency that addresses these kinds of issues known as the Federal Erroneous Retirement Coverage Corrections Act. I put him in touch with them and gave him the instructions on what to do. When we met for his annual review, he proudly showed me his Social Security Statement and said, "Look! They're back." He went and got it fixed, but it was quite threatening because he was close to retirement age, and he was really getting the run around. It just pays to know the right people to go to.

Another strategy is to apply for Social Security at the optimal time. What's the optimal time? It depends on you, and you want to consider your break-even age, your life expectancy, and your income needs.

Another way to maximize your payment is to coordinate spousal benefits. This is a way to really boost your benefits, and is known as "file and suspend." How it works is at the full retirement age   the higher-earning spouse applies for his benefits, and asks that it be suspended. Meanwhile the lower-earning spouse files for the spousal benefits. The higher earning spouse claims his own benefit at age 70.

Let's look at an example of this. Bill and Barbara are both 66. Bill's PIA, his Primary Insurance Amount, is $2,000. Barbara's is $800, which is less than her spousal benefit of $1,000. So, if Bill waits until age 70 to apply, his benefit will go from $2,000 to $2,640. However, Barbara can't claim her Social Security benefit until Bill files for benefits. Thus, their best strategy is for Bill to file for Social Security and suspend at age 66. This entitles his wife, Barbara, to her spousal benefit, while Bill's benefit continues to earn delayed credits.

Another strategy is "claim now, claim more later." Here's how it works. At full retirement age, the higher-earning spouse applies for his spousal benefit only. But his spouse must be receiving the benefit on her record. Then, at age 70, the higher earning spouse now switches to his own higher benefit.

Let's look at an example of this. Paul and Irene are 66. Paul's PIA is $2,000. Irene's is $800. Irene files for her benefit at age 66. Paul files for his spousal benefit at the same time. When Paul turns 70, he switches to his own higher benefit and the result is Paul receives an additional $400.00 a month from age 66 to 70, until he gets his own delayed benefit at age 70.

If you're going to try to do this, remember that the higher-earning spouse may not do this before his full retirement age, so you can't do it at a reduced retirement age of 62. The language to use when applying is that the higher earnings spouse says that he or she is restricting his application to his spousal benefit. That's the key word – "restricting." Only one spouse may do this, so both spouses can't be receiving spousal benefits on each other. This can get fairly involved and it might pay to hire an expert advisor that understands Social Security benefits before making these decisions.

Another strategy for maxing on Social Security is to minimize the taxation of benefits. Up to 85% of your benefits may be taxable, which amounts to a surtax for retirees. They pay taxes going in, and it's very likely that up to 85% of their Social Security benefits may be taxed.

If you are married, filing jointly, and your adjusted gross income, which includes half of your Social Security, is under $32,000, your

Social Security is not subject to tax. If your adjusted gross income is between $32,000 and $44,000, 50% of your Social Security will be taxed. If your adjusted gross income (again, including half of your Social Security income) is over $44,000, 85% of your Social Security benefit will be taxed.

If you're single, the rules are as follows: If your adjusted gross income is under $25,000, zero of your Social Security is taxed. If it's between $25,000 and $34,000, 50% of the Social Security benefit will be taxed. If your adjusted gross income is over $34,000, 85% of your Social Security benefit will be taxed. Most of the federal employees for whom we do planning fall into that bracket

A good way to minimize taxes on Social Security benefits is to reduce any other income with tax advantage investments. If you're not using your money, put it in tax advantage investments, not in municipal bonds, because municipal bonds' interest is actually included in that provisional income that goes into your adjusted gross income for determining whether or not Social Security will be taxed.

Also, anticipate your IRA. Your IRA is tax-deferred, but anticipate your required minimum distributions. They may put you in a higher tax bracket and subject your Social Security benefits to taxation. What you need to do in order to maximize your Social Security is to coordinate your Social Security with your overall retirement income plan.

Will Social Security provide you with enough to live on? Probably not, so consider Social Security as another piece of your retirement income, along with your federal pension, your TSP, and any additional IRAs or Roth IRAs that you have in your investment portfolio.

CHAPTER
9

UNDERSTANDING

MEDICARE

★

There are four parts to Medicare. Part A is hospitalization insurance. Part B is medical insurance. Part C is Medicare Advantage, and Part D is prescription drug coverage.

Part A, or hospitalization insurance, pays for in-patient hospital care. It'll pay for critical access hospitals, skilled nursing facility care up to a limited time, some home healthcare, and hospice care.

You're paying into Part A while you're working; 1.45% of your gross paycheck gets paid into Part A. If you're still working after age 65, you're still going to pay into it, but go ahead and opt-in for Part A, because there's no additional cost for that, since you've been paying into it over your work history. In Part A, in-patient hospital deductible is $1,132. With in-patient hospital co-insurance, you will have to pay $283 a day if you're in the hospital past 60 days, up to 90 days. For a stay longer than 90 days, and between 90 days and 150 days, you'd have to pay co-insurance of $566 a day. When considering these numbers, remember that these days, hospitals are not keeping you in for any longer than absolutely necessary.

For a stay in a skilled nursing facility, your co-insurance is $141.50 a day for stays between 21 and 100 days. If you're in a skilled nursing facility longer than 100 days, Part A won't pay for anything. In fact, Part A insurance for nursing homes is usually not paid, because you have to be receiving skilled care and 97% of people in nursing homes don't require skilled care, but only custodial care.

It's free at age 65, as long as you qualify for Medicare with 40 credits, or your spouse does. People with less than 10 years of Medicare payments will pay a Part A premium.

Part B is your medical insurance. It helps to pay for doctor's services, ambulance services, outpatient hospital care, x-rays, laboratory tests, durable medical equipment and supplies, some home healthcare, and most outpatient services. It also pays for some additional services such as physical and occupational therapy.

For Part B, doctor's services, the deductible is $162 a year. After that deductible, Part B will pay for 80% of this cost. Outpatient hospital treatments are paid the same as doctor's services.

But there is a premium for Part B, based on modified adjusted gross income. The following chart explains how this works, according to how much you make:

Park B Monthly Premium		
	Beneficiaries who file an **individual** tax return with income	Beneficiaries who file a **joint** tax return with income
Your 2012 Part B Monthly Premium Is	**If Your Yearly Income Is**	
$99.90	$85,000 or less	$170,000 or less
$139.90	$85,001-$107,000	$170,001-$214,000
$199.80	$170,001-$160,000	$214,001-$320,000
$259.70	$160,001-$214,000	$320,001-$428,000
$319.70	Above $214,000	Above $428,000

Do I need to take Part B as soon as I'm eligible? The initial enrollment period for Part B is three months before you turn 65, the month you turn 65, and three months after you turn 65. If you're still working, you can delay and not have to pay a penalty for that.

If you're still working, you must enroll in Part B within eight months from the time that you stop working or you're no longer covered by a group plan. If you don't follow these guidelines, you're going to have a 10% penalty or 10% increase in your premium for each year that you were eligible for, but didn't take, Part B.

As a federal employee, do I need Part B? There are pros and cons. Some of the pros are, you may have broader access to out-of-network, and also pay lower co-pays. You can use Medicare if you ever decide to go outside of your HMO network. I've talked to several people that had Medicare plus their FEHB (their Federal Employee Health Benefit insurance) who said it was a Godsend, because they paid minimal out-of-pocket costs for their healthcare.

What are the negatives? It's costly – about $1,400 a year. Blue Cross Standard and Medicare premiums combined for a couple are close to $8,000 a year. That's before you spend a dime on Medicare.

The other disadvantage is that Medicare becomes the primary payer. You may have heard that your physician may not accept Medicare. What we have found is most primary physicians still accept Medicare; however, you may find that the specialists you want to go to will not accept Medicare.

Also, as we mentioned earlier, there is means testing with Medicare Part B, so the higher your income is, the higher your premiums will be (see the chart above).

Third, there is Part C, Medicare Advantage. By joining Medicare Advantage Plan, you generally get all your Medicare benefits through a private insurer. This is something that, as a federal employee, you don't want. You already have your federal employee health benefits, so Part C is something that you won't need or want.

Then there's Part D, the prescription drug coverage. Private companies provide Medicare prescription drug coverage. The average monthly premium in 2011 was $32.34, and there is an annual deductible of $310. Right now, all of the FEHB insurance programs offer prescription drug coverage. If you're enrolled in the FEHB, you don't need part D. But you must join Part D within 63 days if you ever lose your FEHB coverage.

How much will I pay for Part D in 2011? Part D will pay for the first $2,840 of your prescription drugs. You're responsible for the next $4,550 of prescription drug payments (this gap is what's called the "doughnut hole") after which Part D kicks in again and covers your drug costs.

How can I avoid that "doughnut hole" gap? Your FEHB with prescription drug coverage will pay the gap. Again, this is something you'll need to worry about if you lose your FEHB coverage. A way to lessen your prescription costs is to ask your doctor if generic drugs will work for you, then shop around for the best price.

What does Medicare not cover? Medicare doesn't cover your monthly Part B, Part C, or Part D premiums. It doesn't cover deductibles, co-insurance, or co-payments, or outpatient prescription drugs, unless you're enrolled in the plan that provides drug coverage. It doesn't cover routine or annual physicals. Medicare doesn't cover custodial care or cosmetic surgery, hearing aids, vision, foot care, dentures, or dental care.

Something you want to consider is whether or not, as a federal employee, you need Medicare. Only about 10% of federal employees are enrolled in Medicare because they feel that their FEHB coverage is sufficient to meet their needs.

Nothing about your current medical insurance is going to change when you retire, except you're going to be paying for the premiums after tax. While you're employed, you're paying for your medical insurance premiums pre-tax. Everything else remains the same with your FEHB. If you're employed, FEHB is going to be the first to pay your benefits. If you're retired and you have Medicare and FEHB, Medicare is your primary payer.

The period for general enrollment for Medicare, if you didn't enroll during your initial eligibility is from January 1st to March 31st each year. Part D enrollment is November 15th to December 31st.

Last, but not least, is Medicaid. People tend to get Medicare and Medicaid mixed up – but Medicare and Medicaid are very different.

Medicaid is a federal program for low-income, financially needy people, which is set up by the federal government and administered differently in each state. Although you may qualify for and receive coverage from both Medicare and Medicaid, each program has separate eligibility requirements. Being eligible for one program doesn't necessarily mean you're eligible for the other.

Also, Medicaid does pay for some services for which Medicare does not. If you are eligible for Medicaid, Medicaid may pay Medicare deductibles and Medicare premiums. If you're looking for specific information about enrolling in Medicaid, you can contact your state's Medicaid office, or you can visit the website at www.benefits.gov.

If you have or can get both Medicare and Veteran's benefits, you can get treatment under either Medicare A or Medicare D programs. When you see a healthcare provider, you must choose which benefits you're going to use. You must make this choice each time you see a doctor or get healthcare. Medicare can't pay for the same service that was covered by the Veteran's benefit, and your Veteran's benefit can't pay for the same service that was covered by Medicare.

You don't always have to go to a Department of Veterans Affairs Hospital or to a doctor who works with the VA to pay for the service. To get the VA to pay for services, you must go to a VA facility or have the VA authorize services in a non-VA facility. You can get more information on Veteran's benefits by calling your local VA office or the national VA information number at 800-827-1000. You can also visit the VA website, which is www.VA.com. And for more information on Medicare, visit its website at www.medicare.gov.

Keep in mind -- Social Security and Medicare are too important for guesswork. If you need help, seek the advice of an expert.

SECTION

5

DON'T JUST SURVIVE – THRIVE IN RETIREMENT

AN INTRODUCTION

───────────── ✦ ─────────────

S o you've finally qualified for retirement…now what? Just because you have reached the age when you can qualify for an unreduced annuity, or get-out-of-jail-free card, do you really want to – and are you financially and emotionally prepared?

Retirement means entering the next phase of your life. This is an exciting time. Not only do you want to make sure you have planned well to have sufficient income, but you also need to give serious thought to what you want to do during this phase, so that you will not only survive during retirement, but THRIVE! Most baby boomers won't ever really retire. Today's retirees are looking for fulfillment, rather than a rocking chair.

How can you maximize the tools offered through your federal employment to create a strategy for your successful retirement?

CHAPTER
10

WHAT MAKES A SECURE AND
HAPPY RETIREMENT?

You may have attended retirement classes that lay out how your federal benefits will take you into retirement. The reality is that money and your benefits are the second-most important part of retirement planning. You might not expect to hear that from a federal benefits specialist, but the truth is that once your basic needs are met, having more money won't necessarily make you happier. What you will do and who you will be in retirement are much more important than the dollars. Let's take a little pop quiz to help you see what seems to bring current retirees the most satisfaction:

1. Of those who work in retirement, what percentage does so primarily because they want to, not because they need to?
   A) 12%
   B) 37%
   C) 57%
   D) 68%

2. What is the best thing you can do in your prime earning years to make your retirement pleasurable?

   A) Put in overtime so you can pump up your retirement fund.

   B) Put in time at the gym so you can pump up your pecs.

3. Retirees who have only 401Ks are just as satisfied as those with only pension plans.

   A) True

   B) False

4. Most boomers want to live closer to their grandkids in retirement. As for those who have sworn off diaper duty, where do they say they'd be happiest living?

   A) In a college town

   B) In a city

   C) In a foreign country

   D) By the water or beach

5. Once you retire, which of the following is likely to have the biggest effect on your happiness?

   A) The size of your nest egg

   B) Your blood pressure

   C) The number of people who come to your birthday party

   D) A hole in one at Augusta National Golf Club

ANSWERS:

1. **D**: Over half of those who work for the joy of it say they're "very satisfied," versus only 16% of those who do it for the money. The lesson: Save now so that you won't be forced into a job you hate later. Source: Putnam Investments

2. B: Go work out. If you have enough socked away for a moderately comfortable retirement, extra money isn't likely to make much difference. A $10,000 boost in your annual income in retirement raises the probability that you'll be very satisfied by one measly percentage point. Meanwhile, retirees in poor health are 20% more likely to be discontented than those in good health.
Source: Keith Bender Center for Retirement Research

3. **False**; although 401Ks give you more control over investments, they also bring greater uncertainty, and this weighs heavily on the minds of retirees.
Source: Center for Retirement Research

4. **D**: Some 49% want to be by the water. Hawaii may be out of the question for most, given that a 3-bedroom ocean-view home there can easily cost $2 million. However, in Dunedin, Florida, a three-bedroom home goes for a more affordable $200,000. With the money you save, you can visit Junior whenever you want.
Source: Money's "Best Places to Retire"

5. **C**: Turns out, friends are better than gold. The biggest effect on well-being comes from the size of a retiree's social network. It outweighs even health and money. Those with 16 good pals are, on average, far more satisfied with life than those with 10 friends or less.
Source: University of Michigan

SOME THINGS TO CONSIDER
FOR INCOME SECURITY

Could you survive another market downturn like the one we saw in 2000 through 2002? Or 2008? Or even during the Great Depression, especially if you were in or close to retirement? Are you secure that you will have enough income to be able to maintain your desired standard of living throughout your retirement? We're talking about income security. This is not your parent's retirement. The retirement system, following the Great Depression, for many was simple and worry-free. The employee was not responsible for the plan's investment decisions, which resulted in a lack of anxiety. A retirement meant that the retiree would receive a pension check, guaranteed for life. This type of plan is called a "Defined Benefit Plan," and is what your CSRS or FERS annuity is. Under the new retirement system, which I refer to as the "yo-yo" retirement system, you're on your own. With the implementation of FERS in 1987, federal employees became more responsible for managing their own retirement income. It's not better or worse than CSRS – it's just different, and it's putting more and more of that responsibility on you. In addition to defined benefit pensions, your parents could ladder bonds and CDs. But for most retirees today, this method will not create enough income or liquidity to meet their retirement income needs.

Do you want your retirement success to be dependent on how the stock market is doing? Do you want your retirement income dependent on what Ben Bernanke decides to do? Do you have a plan so that taxes will not take the spice out of your retirement? Hopefully, you're going have a long life in retirement. Statistics (from the US Annuity 2000 Mortality Table Society of Actuaries) tell us that, for a couple who are both 65 today, there's a 50 percent chance that one will live to age 92. There's a 25 percent chance that one will live to age 97.

★ ★

"I'm retired – goodbye tension, hello pension."

– Author Unknown

★ ★

In planning your retirement, anticipate rising healthcare costs and don't forget inflation's impact on your future buying power. Be prepared that taxes may take a larger bite out of retirement income, and understand the risks presented by an extended illness and the need for long term care.

CHAPTER 11

MISCONCEPTIONS ABOUT RETIREMENT INCOME

───────────────── ✦ ─────────────────

everal common misconceptions about retirement income need to be dispelled. Misconception number one, created by Wall Street, is the mistaken idea that a secure retirement comes from dividends and interest. The reality is that there's no certainty that Wall Street will be able to provide this. When creating retirement income this way, many retirees are risking short-changing their lifestyles.

Misconception number two is that if your portfolio averages an annual return of 6% and your withdrawal rate is 5%, you don't ever have to worry about running out of money. The reality is that the sequence of returns is going to dictate how much you have in your portfolio. And the sequence of returns is the order of returns realized in a portfolio that could have a significant impact on your retirement assets.

★ ★

"Being rich is having money.

Being wealthy is having time."

– Margaret Bonnano

★ ★

This is an even more dangerous time for your retirement savings, again because of the timing factor. Keep in mind that the example we are about to walk through is just a hypothetical example and does not reflect the actual investment results of any retired person, nor does it illustrate actual market performance.

Let's look at the investment performance of two people who will retire at age 62. First, let's look at Joe Smith who is 62 and retiring now. He has savings of $250,000 and plans to withdraw 5% of his starting account value each year, adjusted annually for 3% inflation. His portfolio averaged a 6% rate of return over a 30-year period.

Three years prior to that, Mary Jones had also retired at the age of 62 with $250,000 in savings. Like Joe, Mary planned to withdraw 5% of her starting account value each year, adjusted annually for 3% inflation. Fast-forward 30 years and she also enjoyed an average annual return of 6% for a 30-year period.

So should we assume that Joe and Mary had the same amount of money at the end of their 30-year period? No, we should not – and that is because of something called the sequence of returns. Here's the outcome: Joe was completely out of money at the age of 77; 15

years into retirement and flat broke. Mary did rather well, and had an account balance of $432,000 after 30 years of retirement. This is important to understand – and also completely out of your control.

How did this happen? Joe unfortunately had the bad luck. Upon his retirement, the stock market went through a downturn. The first year, his account dropped by 18%, followed by a 13% drop in the second year, and an 11% drop in year three.

Mary was luckier with her portfolio. When she decided to retire at the age of 62 with $250,000 in her retirement account, she experienced three positive years early on. Year 1, her portfolio increased by 15%, year two, positive 6%, and year 3, a positive 11% rate of return. Her declines were pretty severe in the later years, but the outcome was that she still had $432,000 of savings after 30 years, where Joe was flat broke by his 15th year. And, both Joe and Mary's portfolios had the same annualized average return of 6%.[5]

Misconception number three is that you can continue to invest in the same way that you did while you were working. The reality is that, during the distribution stage, your portfolio should have protection strategies to overcome volatility, especially when you're taking income. A perfect example of that is what happened back in 2000-2002. If you had an account value of $100,000 and you were in the TSP C fund from September 2000 till September 2002, your account value would have dropped to $55,270. In order to get back up to that $100,000 mark, you would need an 81 percent rate of return. In this example, if you had held on and stayed in that C fund, you would have made that back up.

What if you're taking distribution? Take that same example; you have $100,000, you're in a TSP C fund, and you're taking a distribution of $500 a month. Go through the market downturn from September 2000 through September 2002, and now your account value has dropped all the way down to $42,770. You still need that $500 a month to meet your fixed expenses. So what are you going to do? The likelihood of that portfolio running completely down to zero is pretty high. It's critical to understand that when you're taking income, you have to look at it in a different way. You have to plan much differently than you did when you were in that accumulation phase.

Misconception number four is that the TSP is the best choice for taking income. The reality is that it depends on the individual circumstances. For many people, the TSP is the best choice for taking income. For others, it's not. To give you an example of this – if you are okay taking a certain amount of income from TSP, you're comfortable with the allocation of the funds, and you can live within the restrictions that TSP has regarding taking withdrawals, then you might be perfectly happy leaving it in TSP and staying in these low-cost index funds. Let's assume that you're taking $1,000 a month in withdrawals, and your car breaks down. You call TSP and say, "Can you send me a check for $15,000? I need to get a new car." That's not allowed. If you do that, they're going to make you take out all your money.

What if you're taking out $1,000 a month, then realize you really don't need that much? Come September that extra money is going to put you into the next tax bracket, plus it's going to affect your Social Security and your Medicare premium. You call TSP and say, "Hey, can you stop these automatic payments to my bank account; I don't need anything for the rest of the year." They're going tell you, "No, we can't. We're only allowed to make changes in January."

The decision whether or not to stay in TSP depends on your particular circumstances and needs. The funds are index funds and they're very low cost, but you have to be willing to live within the restrictions. For others, it might better to move that money to an IRA and to look at other investment options. Again, it's imperative that if you do this, you're doing this for the right reasons. You're rolling it into an IRA because you believe it's a more suitable investment strategy, and you can have more flexibility in withdrawing from your TSP. It really depends on the individual situation. You're going to hear, "Stay in TSP, that's the best thing. If someone's recommending that you move it, they're just doing that so they can get a commission." And perhaps in some cases, that's true. On the other hand, you're going to hear, "Get it out of TSP; they don't want your money anyway, that's why there are so many restrictions." Again, it's strictly an individual decision and the only person that can make that decision is you.

★ ★

"Retirement has been a discovery of beauty for me.

I never had the time before to notice the beauty of

my grandkids, my wife, the tree outside my very own

front door ... And the beauty of time itself."

– Hartman Jule

★ ★

Misconception number five is that you're going to need 70% to 80% of your pre-retirement income for retirement. But how is this calculated, and how will you know if you'll have enough? The best way to find out is to complete a full analysis of your income needs and goals, which will give you a much more accurate way of determining your true income need. Typically, federal employees are able to have about the same amount of income in retirement that they bring home while they're working. But you need to take it a step further and remember we have to take other costs into account; inflation, taxes, and the rising costs of healthcare, which are outpacing the overall rate of inflation. It's important to look beyond that first couple of years of retirement and make sure that you're comfortable that your income needs are going to be met.

★ ★

"Wealth is the ability to fully experience life."

– Henry David Thoreau

★ ★

What are some strategies for resolving these misconceptions? First of all, recognize that the biggest fear doesn't change, and that's running out of income. The way you manage the process of creating income has changed, putting more and more of the responsibility on you. You need to be sure that your TSP allocations are right, or that you're moving into the appropriate IRA. You have to make certain that you will have enough income throughout your retirement. It's not the government's job to do that.

You have to analyze your long-term care options, because poor planning for long-term care can wipe out all your goals for your retirement, not only financially but in the emotional strain it creates on you and your family.

Lastly, utilize the tools that are available for creating income. When I work independently with my clients we utilize a variety of tools to help them make sure that they're getting income sufficient to meet their fixed expenses. And whether you work with a financial expert or do it yourself, make sure you utilize the tools that are available for you in managing your TSP and creating income for life.

[5] Rates of return in this example are for illustrative purposes only and do not imply or guarantee that your investments will achieve these results nor do the figures represent the returns of any particular investment. The figures are hypothetical and do not take taxes into account. Actual rates of return on your investments will vary. Investments in securities are subject to investment risk, including possible loss of principal. Prices of securities may fluctuate from time to time and may even become valueless. Before making any investment decision, customers should read and consider all the relevant investment product's offering documents and information. Customers should also seriously consider if the investment is suitable for them by referencing their own financial position, investment objectives, and risks profile before making any investment decision.

CHAPTER 12

WHAT WILL *YOUR* RETIREMENT LOOK LIKE?

There are a variety of things you'll want to consider as you look at thriving in retirement. The professional fulfillment assessment included below will be helpful in helping you recognize the things that have had meaning for you throughout your career. Sometimes a client will tell me that there's nothing they will miss about their workplace. It often turns out that there's a surprising void in retirement that they weren't expecting. This assessment should be helpful in avoiding that unexpected surprise

PROFESSIONAL FULFILLMENT ASSESSMENT

By assessing the amount of personal fulfillment you get from your professional role, you can begin to focus on key areas as you plan for your retirement. Often, people do not realize just how much they get out of certain aspects of their working careers – and they fail to account for them in their retirement plans.

The survey below assesses sources of fulfillment before retirement and reveals which of those sources could diminish or go away. Armed with this revelation, you will have a much better chance of planning a rewarding retirement.

Fulfillment comes from finding satisfaction in areas of your life you regard as important. Consider your life when working in your career. Evaluate potential sources of fulfillment by filling in the appropriate answer for each topic.

Satisfaction – How satisfied or dissatisfied have you been in this area?
Importance – How important is this area to you, overall?
How Much from Work? – Approximately how much does this area depend on your job or career?

1. RECOGNITION –
Having people acknowledge and appreciate what you do, e.g. applause

Satisfaction
O Completely Satisfied   O Mostly Satisfied   O Partly Satisfied
O Slightly Satisfied   O Not Satisfied

Importance
O Extremely Important   O Very Important   O Important
O Slightly Important   O Not Important

Percent from work

○ None ○ A Little ○ Some ○ Most ○ All

2. TIME STRUCTURE – Having responsibilities, duties, and commitments that organize your days

Satisfaction

○ Completely Satisfied ○ Mostly Satisfied ○ Partly Satisfied
○ Slightly Satisfied ○ Not Satisfied

Importance

○ Extremely Important ○ Very Important ○ Important
○ Slightly Important ○ Not Important

Percent from work ○ None ○ A Little ○ Some ○ Most ○ All

3. PURPOSE – Knowing that what you do has meaning, value, and significance for yourself and/or others

Satisfaction

○ Completely Satisfied ○ Mostly Satisfied ○ Partly Satisfied
○ Slightly Satisfied ○ Not Satisfied

Importance

○ Extremely Important ○ Very Important ○ Important
○ Slightly Important ○ Not Important

Percent from work

○ None ○ A Little ○ Some ○ Most ○ All

4. HELPING OTHERS – Providing services, nurturing, mentoring, assisting, and supporting people

Satisfaction
○ Completely Satisfied ○ Mostly Satisfied ○ Partly Satisfied
○ Slightly Satisfied ○ Not Satisfied

Importance
○ Extremely Important ○ Very Important ○ Important
○ Slightly Important ○ Not Important

Percent from work
○ None ○ A Little ○ Some ○ Most ○All

5. COMMUNITY – Actively participating in civic projects, associations, organizations

Satisfaction
○ Completely Satisfied ○ Mostly Satisfied ○ Partly Satisfied
○ Slightly Satisfied ○ Not Satisfied

Importance
○ Extremely Important ○ Very Important ○ Important
○ Slightly Important ○ Not Important

Percent from work
○ None ○ A Little ○ Some ○ Most ○All

6. FAMILY – Enjoying time with loved ones; your mate, associations, organizations

Satisfaction
○ Completely Satisfied ○ Mostly Satisfied ○ Partly Satisfied
○ Slightly Satisfied ○ Not Satisfied

Importance
○ Extremely Important ○ Very Important ○ Important
○ Slightly Important ○ Not Important

Percent from work
○ None ○ A Little ○ Some ○ Most ○All

7. PROFESSIONAL AFFILIATION – Regular interaction with others involved in the kind of work you do

Satisfaction
○ Completely Satisfied ○ Mostly Satisfied ○ Partly Satisfied
○ Slightly Satisfied ○ Not Satisfied

Importance
○ Extremely Important ○ Very Important ○ Important
○ Slightly Important ○ Not Important

Percent from work
○ None ○ A Little ○ Some ○ Most ○All

8. MENTAL CHALLENGE – Intellectual excitement; pursuits that stretch your mind and keep you sharp

Satisfaction
O Completely Satisfied   O Mostly Satisfied   O Partly Satisfied
O Slightly Satisfied   O Not Satisfied

Importance
O Extremely Important   O Very Important   O Important
O Slightly Important   O Not Important

Percent from work
O None   O A Little   O Some   O Most   OAll

9. PHYSICAL ACTIVITY – Regular exercise for recreation or fitness, such as walking, yard-work, or a sport

Satisfaction
O Completely Satisfied   O Mostly Satisfied   O Partly Satisfied
O Slightly Satisfied   O Not Satisfied

Importance
O Extremely Important   O Very Important   O Important
O Slightly Important   O Not Important

Percent from work
O None   O A Little   O Some   O Most   O All

10. INFLUENCE – Exercising power, authority, leadership or status through what you do

Satisfaction
O Completely Satisfied   O Mostly Satisfied   O Partly Satisfied
O Slightly Satisfied   O Not Satisfied

Importance
O Extremely Important   O Very Important   O Important
O Slightly Important   O Not Important

Percent from work
O None   O A Little   O Some   O Most   O All

11. COLLABORATION – Cooperating in joint efforts; working and/or playing as a member of a team, committee, or group

Satisfaction
O Completely Satisfied   O Mostly Satisfied   O Partly Satisfied
O Slightly Satisfied   O Not Satisfied

Importance
O Extremely Important   O Very Important   O Important
O Slightly Important   O Not Important

Percent from work
O None   O A Little   O Some   O Most   OAll

12. EARNING – Generating income from your efforts; getting paid for what you do

Satisfaction
O Completely Satisfied O Mostly Satisfied O Partly Satisfied
O Slightly Satisfied O Not Satisfied

Importance
O Extremely Important O Very Important O Important
O Slightly Important O Not Important

Percent from work
O None O A Little O Some O Most O All

13. CREATIVE EXPRESSION – Producing artistic, innovative, original ideas or works

Satisfaction
O Completely Satisfied O Mostly Satisfied O Partly Satisfied
O Slightly Satisfied O Not Satisfied

Importance
O Extremely Important O Very Important O Important
O Slightly Important O Not Important

Percent from work
O None O A Little O Some O Most O All

14. ENVIRONMENTS – Function, pleasing places that give needed comfort, solitude, interaction, and/or stimulation

Satisfaction
O Completely Satisfied O Mostly Satisfied O Partly Satisfied
O Slightly Satisfied O Not Satisfied

Importance
O Extremely Important O Very Important O Important
O Slightly Important O Not Important

Percent from work
O None O A Little O Some O Most OAll

15. INDEPENDENT ACCOMPLISHMENT – Individual achievement through sustained, personal effort

Satisfaction
O Completely Satisfied O Mostly Satisfied O Partly Satisfied
O Slightly Satisfied O Not Satisfied

Importance
O Extremely Important O Very Important O Important
O Slightly Important O Not Important

Percent from work
O None O A Little O Some O Most O All

16. SOCIAL CONNECTION – Networking; staying in touch, informed and up-to-date via personal contacts

Satisfaction
O Completely Satisfied   O Mostly Satisfied   O Partly Satisfied
O Slightly Satisfied   O Not Satisfied

Importance
O Extremely Important   O Very Important   O Important
O Slightly Important   O Not Important

Percent from work
O None   O A Little   O Some   O Most   O All

17. TRAVEL – Journeying to visit (or re-visit) distant, enjoyable places

Satisfaction
O Completely Satisfied   O Mostly Satisfied   O Partly Satisfied
O Slightly Satisfied   O Not Satisfied

Importance
O Extremely Important   O Very Important   O Important
O Slightly Important   O Not Important

Percent from work
O None   O A Little   O Some   O Most   OAll

18. SPIRITUALITY – Participating in church, worship, religion, spiritual practice, or introspection

Satisfaction
○ Completely Satisfied ○ Mostly Satisfied ○ Partly Satisfied
○ Slightly Satisfied ○ Not Satisfied

Importance
○ Extremely Important ○ Very Important ○ Important
○ Slightly Important ○ Not Important

Percent from work
○ None ○ A Little ○ Some ○ Most ○All

19. SELF-DEVELOPMENT – Life-long learning; education, training, or study

Satisfaction
○ Completely Satisfied ○ Mostly Satisfied ○ Partly Satisfied
○ Slightly Satisfied ○ Not Satisfied

Importance
○ Extremely Important ○ Very Important ○ Important
○ Slightly Important ○ Not Important

Percent from work
○ None ○ A Little ○ Some ○ Most ○All

20. FRIENDSHIP – Spending time with your friends and companions

Satisfaction
O Completely Satisfied   O Mostly Satisfied   O Partly Satisfied
O Slightly Satisfied   O Not Satisfied

Importance
O Extremely Important   O Very Important   O Important
O Slightly Important   O Not Important

Percent from work
O None   O A Little   O Some   O Most   OAll

How accurately does your Professional Fulfillment Assessment reflect the overall fulfillment you have gained from work?

How well does the assessment capture the balance you have kept between work and the rest of your life?

When away from work longer than usual, what do you miss most?

What are the sources of emotional and intellectual fulfillment that you have gotten from work – or hoped to get – that you want to include in your retirement?

What kinds of non-work fulfillment do you want?

Of all the sources of fulfillment listed in the assessment, which ones do you want to focus on in retirement?

WHERE TO LIVE?

One of the important things you'll want to consider is where you're going to live in retirement. Although a lot of people report that they are going to stay right where they are, about an equal number report that they're going to move and live somewhere else. Among the things that you'll want to consider when you're deciding where to live in retirement is the lifestyle that you're looking for. Do you want a fast-paced lifestyle, the opportunity to go to arts or educational events, a very busy community – or are you looking for a more laid-back lifestyle? Are you looking for a place where there are lots of outdoor activities?

You want to make sure that you're matching up your expectations with what the community you choose actually offers. You'll also want to consider the healthcare options within that community. You're going to have great health benefits that you get to take with you into retirement, but you want to be sure that you'll have access to the kinds of health delivery systems that your health insurance is going to partner up with nicely.

You'll also want to know about the housing and the real estate market in these communities. Is it going to cost you more to live in a place where you want to live in retirement, or less? Many people assume that they're going to live in a place that will cost them less; that the housing they're planning to relocate to will be less expensive than where they're starting out. In recent years, that hasn't always been the case, but it is highly dependent on the actual location you're considering.

You'll probably want to consider the climate where you're looking to move. For instance, think about whether you want to be in a place that has four seasons, versus a place where it's warm year-round. That's why so many retirees end up in California and Florida. What are the taxes like? There are some states that actually have no state income tax; Alaska, Florida, Nevada, New Hampshire, South Dakota, Tennessee, Texas, Washington, and Wyoming (While New Hampshire and Tennessee don't tax wage income, they do tax interest and dividends. The applicable rates are 5% and 6%, respectively.)

When you consider a state that has no income tax, you're thinking, "Oh, well, at least I'll have a little extra money to spend there." However, remember that every community has certain fixed expenses that they incur, and one way or the other, they have to cover those expenses, whether it's through a state income tax, through sales tax, or through property taxes. The states that have no sales tax tend to have higher property taxes. Ultimately, you're probably going to pay about the same amount in total taxes.

There are lots of ways you can find the best places to live in retirement; if you simply Google "best places to live in retirement," you'll get a whole long list. Kiplinger's magazine and Money magazine both put out yearly publications on this topic, as does Yahoo, so you can review their criteria and match them against your needs and wants.

According to usnews.com, the 10 best places to retire in 2012 are: Flagstaff, AZ, Boone, NC, Traverse City, MI, Walnut Creek, CA, Ithaca, NY, Lincoln, NE, Pittsburg, PA, Port Charlotte, FL, Pittsfield, MA, and Santa Fe, NM. Clearly, this is a very diverse group, so keep in mind that their criteria might not be the same as your criteria. It's just a place to start.

WORKING IN RETIREMENT

Some baby boomers tell us that they're going to get a job in retirement. They say, "When I stop working for the federal government, I'm going to get a 'fun job.'" There are several reasons federal employees decide to work in retirement. They may need the money to supplement the income that they're going to have from their federal pension and what they can create from their TSP and Social Security, if they have access to it. They may want to wait to take their Social Security until later when the value of that Social Security benefit is higher, so they decide to work in those interim years after they retire from the federal government doing a part-time job, or even something completely different from than what they were doing.

A lot of people come back to work for the federal government as contractors, or go out and become consultants doing exactly the kind of work they were doing when they were federal employees. Consulting is an interesting option. There are a lot of private companies interested in hiring federal employees who have the experience to help them navigate the complexity of the federal government from the inside.

How do you find the best job in retirement? Well, if you're thinking about simply leaving the federal government and going to work in another full-time job, you might be better off staying where you are. If you are not comfortable or not happy in the agency you're in, it may be possible to move to another agency. If you're going to continue to work a full-time job, it could be challenging for you to

---

find a job that would offer you the same pay, continue to increase your pension, plus allow you to add to a plan like a Thrift Savings Plan.

You can also look for a part-time job in either your current profession or something new. You might work as a temporary employee, especially if you're not sure just what it is that you want to do. There are employers who look to bring on temporary seasonal workers, so it gives you a chance to try before you buy. Perhaps you've always thought you'd love to work in a pet store, in the flower shop or at the golf course. This gives you a chance to go in and try it out, and find out whether that's really something that's a good fit for your personality.

You can also use government and community programs. There are a variety of resources for retirees to help them get back into the workforce or to help them remain useful members within the community.

There are some people who simply don't feel fulfilled unless they're contributing something by working. Many federal employees say, "I've been working since I was 14 or 15 years old and the idea of just stopping because I'm eligible to retire feels very uncomfortable." We know that people who can ease into retirement – who go from working 40 hours a week to 32, or down to 24 – make that transition much more easily as opposed to going from 40 hours a week to zero.

Another reason that federal employees may want retirement jobs is because their social life is connected to their work life, and they're used to having most of their friends in the workplace. There is also the fear of a different lifestyle, and people are putting off that shift to retirement because they aren't exactly sure what it's going to look like. Some federal employees spend their whole careers watching the countdown clock - that gently ticking clock that tells them how many years, months, and days they have until retirement. They've been waiting for 30 years for this event. There are others who didn't really start to pay attention to retirement until they were within a few months or a year of it.

While hitting retirement's finish line can be very exciting, for some people it feels more like a cliff than a finish line, because it's a little scary. You don't know what's on the other side of that line. You know what it's like to get up and go to work every day when someone else is setting your schedule. Now, when you're setting your own schedule and you decide what you're going to do, it becomes a little more daunting.

In the first month that you're retired, what's the thing you want to do most? We always take a survey at our retirement courses and ask that question. The number one answer? Sleep. There must be a lot of sleep-deprived people out there who are thinking, "I'm going to put it off now. I'm going to continue to get up early, go to bed late, but when I retire, I am sleeping." If you find that's your answer, you're not alone.

FOR A GOOD CAUSE - VOLUNTEERING

One of the top things that retirees report that they want do is to volunteer. When we talk about volunteering, we encourage you to volunteer wisely. We talked about time management being the most important issue that you're going to have to deal with in retirement (especially early in retirement), because you're now the master of your own clock. No one's telling you when you have to get up, when you have to be at work, how many days off you get, or when your holidays are, so now you really have the opportunity and the responsibility to manage your time. If one of the things you determine that you want to do in retirement is to volunteer for a cause that's important to you, make sure that you take your time management seriously. Nonprofit organizations are struggling mightily for contributions and to get good people to work in their organizations. When you put your name out there as being available to work for them, you will literally have your calendar filled before you know what's hit you. They will line up to take advantage of your availability. That may end up with you saying, "I feel like I'm working 40 hours a week," because you find yourself overwhelmed with volunteer opportunities.

You probably have heard some of your retired friends, neighbors or family members say, "I'm busier now than when I was working." Hopefully because you're looking at this plan ahead of time, you're going to take the opportunity to consciously manage your time, so that you don't end up overwhelmed. Don't let someone take your hard-earned downtime away from you.

Take the time to identify what causes and issues are important to you. Consider what skills you have to offer. One of the things you'll want to do, as you determine those agencies or nonprofit organizations that you want to work with, is to put together a little résumé, not necessarily based on all of your work experience but on the things that you would like to do in the volunteer realm – because if you simply go in and say, "I have time to volunteer," you could end up stuffing and licking envelopes and not enabling the non-profit to take advantage of your skills. It's a common mistake for people not to tell the volunteer organization about their skills, and the way they can best serve the organization. You have to do a little bit of self-marketing, unless of course you're happy stuffing envelopes. If you're happy to become the Jack of all Trades or the Gal Friday for an organization, that's fine, but if you have specific things you want to do, you have to make sure that you let them know that. If you're willing to learn something new, let the volunteer organization know that, as well. Combine your goals of learning to do something new with the time that you have on your hands to help those organizations out.

Finally, make sure that you don't over commit your schedule. You want to leave yourself time to enjoy your retirement.

★ ★

"Find something that you're really interested

in doing in your life, and commit yourself to

excellence. Do the best you can."

– Chris Evert

★ ★

Some of the places that you can consider volunteering? Look at the familiar nonprofits, of course, but also think outside the box. Look at virtual volunteering. There are lots of things that you can do online. If you have great computer skills, there are things that you can do right at home to help an organization, without ever having to go into their offices.

Look at daycare centers, public schools, or your local library. As we see the budgets cut for these kinds of organizations, they are desperate for people to help them. If you have great skills in math, for example, you could help tutor middle school or high school kids in trigonometry or calculus. It's great for you, because it's good for your brain, and we know that teaching keeps those neural pathways open. It's also great for the kids to get that one-on-one attention or have the opportunity to get help in a smaller setting.

Look at animal shelters, museums and galleries, Neighborhood Watch, and community theaters. Look at the airport - many airports utilize volunteers to work as greeters and answer travelers' questions.

Meals on Wheels always needs drivers. Soup kitchens need servers, stockers, sometimes even seasonal help in gardens. If you have a talent for singing or playing a musical instrument, you might look at the community choir or the community symphony, or consider volunteering to entertain at a retirement home. There are lots of opportunities, more opportunities than hours you have in the day, so having a plan prior to retirement can help you to be selective in the beginning.

* *

Wait six months before you make a firm commitment to take on any of these things. That doesn't mean that you're not going to take an opportunity to be part of a fundraising committee or a special event, but if you can go six months so you're comfortable in your schedule and you can see what kind of time you really have, you'll be more successful in managing that time.

* *

BE A LIFE-LONG LEARNER

One of the other common things that federal employees do in retirement is to make a passion out of continuing to learn. What are those things that you want to make sure that you're always involved in, and that you're continually interested to learn about? It's proven that those who are lifelong learners have a greater sense of optimism and a lower chance of dementia, so whatever your interests are, now is the time to dive in. If you have always wanted to learn more about philosophy, you've wanted to take a cooking class, or learn a foreign language, now's the time.

Maybe you're interested in classical literature. Maybe you just want to get up to speed on computers and the whole technology thing. Lots of people like to take up genealogy, and research their family history. You might enjoy an art appreciation class, or learning more about wine. There are endless possibilities to continue your learning and promote your lifelong learner title.

PUT ON YOUR TRAVELING SHOES

Once they're all caught up on their sleep, the next thing that retirees nationwide report that they really want to do is … travel. How can you do that on a budget and make the most use of your travel dollars?

Part of the fun of traveling, if that is something that you want to do, is deciding where you want to go – and the sky should be the limit! Don't eliminate something from this initial list of where you'd like to travel, whether it's Africa, Europe, Disney World, New York City, the Caribbean, put it on your list. Don't eliminate it simply because you think, "That might be too expensive," because we're going to give you lots of great resources to help you manage the costs.

Remember that, in the past, the times that you were able to travel and go on vacation were also the times that everyone else was able to go on vacation. That translates to higher airfares, higher hotel rates, and bigger crowds. But now, unlike those people who are still working, you have the gift of time. You can choose when you're going go, and traveling in the low season can make your trip much less expensive, even to very nice places. Below is a web address that will take you to a great travel resource guide:

http://franklinplanning.com/services.html

Included in this travel resource guide are money-saving tips to help you vacation better. How do you get the best deals on golf? How do you get the best deals on theater tickets if you're going to New York or Las Vegas? There are lots of great resources for you to help you figure out where the best deals are on everything, from your actual travel plans to where you're going eat dinner, so check it out and make those travel dreams come true.

Another way to save real money on outings is to buy entertainment coupon books. You probably all have the neighborhood kids who come to your door to sell you this entertainment book and you're thinking, "I don't want to use coupons," but these are actually a great bargain. You'll find that they will pay for themselves 10 times over or more. There are some other great resources online, too, for saving money on dining out. Restaurant.com and Groupon are both very popular, and you can use these same resources when you're traveling, too.

THINKING ABOUT RETIRING ABROAD?

About 5% of federal pre-retirees ask questions like, "What happens to my federal pension if I retire abroad?," or "What happens with my health coverage if I retire abroad?" As we see the cost of retirement continuing to increase in the U.S., more and more people are looking at those places that truly are less expensive, like Mexico, Costa Rica, South America, or Southeast Asia. Some people say they're going to join the Peace Corps now that they've retired, which is a very inexpensive way to live abroad if you're interested in living a simple lifestyle within a foreign community that combines volunteer work with a travel experience.

A couple of the issues around retiring abroad: Your health coverage typically will cover you while you're abroad on a limited basis. You're probably going to have to get some other type of coverage, depending on whether you are considered an ex-patriot and keep your U.S. citizenship, or whether you obtain dual citizenship.

If you're no longer using your federal health benefits, you're going to use the health benefits in the country where you're going. You want to make sure that you suspend your FEHB coverage. Don't cancel it. You don't have to pay for it while it's suspended. Use the benefits of the country you're in, then if you ever want or need to come back to the United States, you can simply reinstate those health benefits.

FOR BETTER OR WORSE,
BUT NOT FOR LUNCH

If they are married, a common question that people have as they move into retirement is, "Should we retire together?" Consider when the last time was that you spent 24 hours a day, 7 days a week, 365 days a year, with your spouse? That would probably be never, and now you're literally going to be thrown together, full-time, in your house. By talking through some of these things together ahead of time, you can determine that you don't always have to be right next to each other, doing the same thing. Make sure that you're communicating both the positive aspects of spending time together, as well as your frustrations.

Have a purpose for what you're going to do together. Create some structure around those things that you're going to do together, but you also each need to have your own community. Be an individual. Don't simply become a part of "we." You still want to have your individuality.

Work on a budget together, because you may have very different ideas about how you're going to spend those retirement dollars that you'll be living on now. Explore interests together that you didn't have time for prior to retirement. Making a plan ahead of time will help resolve a lot of those conflicts before they ever happen.

Ron and Loretta decided that they were going to retire together. They were both federal employees and they were both high performers in their jobs, so I was a little concerned about the two of them alone together for 24 hours a day, but they did a great job. When they retired, they decided together that they each wanted to do a little consulting on the side, which allowed them to spend time away from each other and still be that independent person that they were while they were working, but with fewer hours. It also gave them a few extra bucks early in retirement, which allowed them to travel and take some trips together that they'd always wanted to do. After the first year in retirement, they reported, "We made it work!

MAKE YOUR BUCKET LIST

This chapter started with a professional fulfillment assessment, about looking back throughout your career and identifying the things that you enjoyed during that time. Now we're going to do another little worksheet, about the things you've always wanted to do and things that you're doing now that you would like to do more of. You might have started doing them before you retired, but you want to make sure that you continue them in retirement. It's called, Dream Forward, but it's really your "bucket list."

If you remember the movie of that name that starred Jack Nicholson and Morgan Freeman, this odd couple was forced into making a bucket list of all the things they wanted to do before they died, because they both had terminal illnesses. The premise of the movie was, of course, don't wait until you're diagnosed with something awful to do the things you really want to do.

You get to determine which of these things you're going to make sure you don't miss along the way; make a to-do list prior to retirement.

DREAM FORWARD

Thinking of things you've always wanted to do – or what you're doing now and hope to continue – will have a key role in your retirement. You may recall some and discover others. Talk with people close to you who may remind you of something you always wanted to do.

1. List one of the activities you are enjoying now and want to continue.

_____

2. List an activity with important people in your life that you hope to sustain.

_____

3. List an activity that you've really wanted to do that you haven't gotten around to.

_____

4. List an interest you yearn to pursue.

_____

5. List one of the skills and talents you wish to develop.

_____

6. List one of the things you hope to accomplish.

_____

7. List a person you dream of knowing or knowing better.

_____

8. List one of the things you want to learn about.

_____

9. List a role you might like to explore.

_____

10. List one of the ways you would like to contribute, make a difference or be remembered.

_____

11. List one of the places you want to go.

_____

12. What are you doing now that you'd do differently in the future?

_____

13. List one other significant dream.

_____

GET ORGANIZED

★ ★

"The question isn't at what age I want to retire,

it's at what income."

– George Foreman

★ ★

Those people who go into retirement with a plan report being 60% more satisfied at the end of their first year of retirement than those who had no plan and just decided to wing it.

Make sure that all your beneficiary forms are updated. This is part of that process of putting all of your important papers in place. Update your estate plan if you haven't done so within the last three years.

✦ ✦

"Fast is fine, but accuracy is everything."

– Wyatt Earp

✦ ✦

If you don't have a computer at home, you may want to consider getting one because that's going be your lifeline to the world. You may not have needed one at home because you've used the computer at the office, but what you'll find is that you'll feel pretty isolated without it.

Make sure you have your emergency fund created. You want to have six months' worth of expenses in this emergency fund. Remember that initially you're not going to get your full retirement amount from OPM. There will be a few months' lag time in which you're only getting a partial payment, so you want to make sure that worrying about money isn't the first thing you end up doing in retirement. Prepare a budget, so you have an expectation of both what's coming in and what you're going to spend.

If you plan to move, have a strategy for doing that. When are you going to move – immediately after you retire, or at some point down the line? How are you going to put your house on the market?

All of these things need to be part of a list, which is an important part of your retirement strategy. In more than 10 years of helping federal employees retire, never, not once, has someone come back to me and said, "I shouldn't have retired. I wish I would've worked longer." There can be some challenges in figuring out what you're going do, but those challenges are not so daunting that you'll wish you were still on the job.

You've made it to the end! Hopefully, this book has helped you gain insights, learn more about your benefits, and be a little less intimidated about your benefits and retirement.

"Twenty years from now, you will be more disappointed by the things you didn't do than by the ones that you did do, so throw off the bow lines, sail away from the safe harbor, catch the trade winds in your sails. Explore, dream, discover."

– Mark Twain

SOURCES

Office of Personnel Management, *www.opm.gov*

Thrift Savings Plan, *www.tsp.gov*

Internal Revenue Service, *www.irs.gov*

Social Security Administration, *www.ssa.gov*

Medicare, *www.medicare.gov*

CPSIA information can be obtained at www.ICGtesting.com
Printed in the USA
BVOW010418080512

289682BV00009B/20/P